D0884645

DISCARDED

New Aspects of Politics

UNIVERSITY OF WINNIPEG
LIBRARY
515 Portage Avenue
Winnipeg, Manitoba R3B 2E9

JA
71
.M4
1970

New Aspects of Politics

Charles E. Merriam

Third Edition, Enlarged
With a Foreword by Barry D. Karl

The University of Chicago Press, Chicago and London

Standard Book Number: 226–52061–7
Library of Congress Catalog Card Number: 77-114809

The University of Chicago Press, Chicago 60637
The University of Chicago Press, Ltd., London

Copyright 1925, 1931 by The University of Chicago
Introduction ©1970 by The University of Chicago
All rights reserved. Third Edition published 1970
Printed in the United States of America

Contents

Foreword by Barry D. Karl

For roughly a quarter of a century, in a period brutally scarred by the end of one world war and the beginning of another, the University of Chicago served as a center of innovation for an American social science which had as its ultimate goal the direct application of scientific intelligence to social problems. And it was to such an active, reforming social science that many in the younger generation of American intellectuals looked to preserve, and then restore, prosperity; to preserve, and then defend, the peace of the world; and to preserve, and then extend, the values long associated with democracy in Western civilization. That the forces of change were opening cultural vistas dominated by, yet virtually excluded from, that civilization was not sufficiently sensed to shake the certitude or shatter the relentless optimism which had sustained progressive reform in America. That it was a period which threatened optimism was clear enough to all observers of the attacks upon democracy abroad; but buoyed by an intellectual leadership which had battled for progressivism under Theodore Roosevelt and Woodrow Wilson and which would be convinced of the rebirth of that leadership in Franklin Roosevelt, the optimism was, for a time at least, preserved.

In the field of political science in particular the name "Chicago school" came to describe a movement which has continued to be traceable in generations of career lines which radiate from Chicago in the 1920s and 30s. Charles E. Merriam was the prophet of that movement. *New Aspects of Politics* was the book of prophecy. When it appeared in 1925, it was an invitation to the future.

To the generation of contemporaries which perused the pages of the small volume, it was by no means totally unfamiliar, a fact which was one of the crucial elements of its success. Since the Christmas meetings of the American Political Science Association in 1920, the already well-known Merriam had begun to assume a status in the profession somewhat different from that accorded him for the previous two decades. In addition to his professorship at the University of Chicago—one might have said "in spite of it"—Merriam's career had come to be rooted in progressive Republican politics. Known to readers of *LaFollette's Weekly Magazine* as "the Woodrow Wilson of the West," he stood among a notable group of men whom his generation applauded as "scholar-politicians," a collection in which men like Merriam's teacher, William

A. Dunning, included Theodore Roosevelt and Henry Cabot Lodge. The backlash of World War I progressivism, among other things, ended Merriam's political career; and with a virtually humiliating defeat in the mayoral primaries in Chicago in 1919, a sharp and painful contrast to his previous ascendance in Chicago politics, he moved into a new phase of professional activity.

The opening attack was a paper entitled "The Present State of the Study of Politics," which seemed intended as the announcement of a sharp break in his own approach to the study of politics. "The original plan of this paper," he began in a skillful variation of the politician's tearing up of the prepared text, "included a general survey and critique of the leading tendencies in the study of politics during the last thirty or forty years. . . . It would have been an interesting and perhaps a useful task." To those familiar with his book *American Political Ideas* which had just appeared in September of 1920, the search for a reversal of field might have been a bit puzzling. That book had had as its subtitle, "Studies in the Development of American Political Thought 1865–1917," and had been in some ways the sort of survey he was now rejecting. "This task was abandoned, however," he continued, "and reserved for another occasion, as it became evident that no such survey could be condensed within reasonable limits. It seemed that our common purpose might be better served by a different type of analysis, aiming at the reconstruction of the methods of political study and the attainment of larger results alike in the theoretical and the practical fields." And he concluded with a call for "more adequate equipment for collection and analysis of political material; more adequate organization of the political prudence of our profession; the broader use of the instruments of social observation in statistics, and of the analytical technique and results of psychology; . . . more organization of our technical research, and its coordination with other and closely allied fields of inquiry." His peroration had the eloquence and tone which would, within the next few years, become a kind of trademark as it alternated with his familiar political banter. "Science is a great cooperative enterprise in which many intelligences must labor together. There must always be wide scope for the spontaneous and unregimented activity of the individual, but the success of the expedition is conditioned upon some general plan of organization. Least of all can there be anarchy in social science, or chaos in the theory of political order." Charles Merriam was forty-four years old. Leadership in the reorganization of his profession was ahead of him, and his hat was in the ring.

Although some would recall it in later years as a lonesome clarion before an audience of devoted-to-the-death constitutionalists and metaphysical moral theorists, Merriam's was by no means the first or the only call for a new political science. In many important respects, the Chicago school then being formed was destined from the beginning to be an offshoot of the Columbia school of Merriam's teachers, John W. Burgess and William A. Dunning, as well as of Francis Lieber who had preceded them. Merriam's refusal of Dunning's Lieber professorship at Columbia in 1923 shifted important aspects of the logical continuity of an American school of political thought to Chicago. His chief reason for this refusal was important. His commitment to Chicago as a whole culture and a political way of life and the deep involvement of that commitment in his efforts to define a science of politics made a move impossible. Indeed, the delicate balance between political activism and political theory was perhaps what gave his voice the particular quality it had in 1920 to a generation whose range of attachments to progressive reform and scientific purity was as complex as his own.

It was not because the basic call was so different from what numerous other postwar social scientists were demanding, but because there was a quality in the way Merriam put his demand—a breadth and inclusiveness—which gave it greater appeal, if not greater clarity. In times of great intellectual change and critical reexamination of traditional hypotheses, a finely honed clarity may be divisive—a useful technique for sharpening awareness of fundamental differences, but unsettling to the search for communal effort; and communal effort was one of the essentials of Merriam's approach. In seeking it, he frequently had to emphasize a community of diverse ideas, even at the expense of clarity. That was not scientific, to be sure, but it was very political.

In the December meetings in 1921 he repeated his appeal in an informal statement. He cited Aristotle as a scientist dependent upon a community of researchers for his work, but dependent, too, on the financial and political support of Alexander the Great; and he called attention to the necessity of finding funds for the building up of collections of equipment for scientific research and the financing of the time of research workers. That, too, was an endeavor familiar to Merriam as a progressive reformer in a city whose well-to-do citizenry could be persuaded to support "scientific" reform studies. It was in fact the way Merriam had gained the kind of experience which he was now pressing on the profession.

Dunning was president of the American Political Science Association that year, and his appointment of a Committee on Political Research with Merriam as its chairman launched a program of events which placed Merriam in the center of the movement for a science of politics. A progress report presented to the association by the end of the next year provided the first full survey of the nature and extent of political research in the United States. Between 1923 and 1925 yearly meetings of a National Conference on the Science of Politics, called for by Arnold Bennett Hall at the 1922 meeting of the association, sought to explore in much more detail the various areas of working relationship between and among the social sciences; but that endeavor died for lack of financial support. As the initial effort to bring the broad range of new social scientists together, it also bore the brunt of the discovery of how deep doctrinal dispute could be—between those who sought immediate political involvement as the purpose of social research and those who demanded an absolute, objective distance from the turmoils of politics; between those

committed to the elaboration of a historical continuity in political and social development and
those who saw history as the restrictive past whose
destruction would have to precede the opening up
of the future; between quantification and intuition,
the older professionals of the city research bureaus
and the newer professionals of the universities, the
elitists who saw industrial society moving in the
direction of a more useful and fixed order and the
neo-Jacksonians who saw elitism as the direct
threat to democratic self-government. The lack of
funding may not have been without its relation to
the level of dispute generated by the search for
science.

It is unlikely that Merriam could have learned
as rapidly as he did the utilities of his own techniques without those conferences. During that same
period he managed to find more than adequate resources for his own research, that of colleagues and
students at the University of Chicago, and, by the
end of the period, for a sizeable portion of the
national community of social scientists. The founding of the Social Science Research Council in 1923
with Rockefeller support; the funding of the Local
Community Research Committee at the University of Chicago, which backed research programs
as varied in their relation to "local community"

as voting behavior in Chicago and international law; and the formation of the Spelman Fund of the Rockefeller Foundation under Merriam's control, all reflected virtual confirmations of Merriam's effective leadership in the profession. The Hanover Conferences of the Social Science Research Council throughout the period provided a remarkably efficient meeting ground for the exchange of ideas and the elaboration of research projects for future support.

In some very crucial respects, *New Aspects of Politics* is a uniquely accurate representation of the political art which underlay Merriam's political science. Its defects as a book, are, in a manner of speaking, Merriam's virtues as a professional leader; and there is, as a result, considerably more to it than meets the mind. In argument and text the book is a distillation of the basic points one would find in *American Political Ideas* (1920); in Merriam's contribution to *Political Theories, Recent Times*, which he edited in 1924 with Harry Elmer Barnes; in the published reports of the Committee on Political Research; and in the papers and conference remarks he delivered to the profession from 1921 to 1924. It lacks "The Present State of the Study of Politics," as well as the presidential address of 1925, "Progress in Political Research."

Both essays have been added to this edition because they indicate the beginning and the peak of this period of his influence.

Chapter by chapter the book casts a protective canopy over every conceivable contemporary canon of social thought. The only real sins are willful ignorance and dogmatism, although corruption, the familiar foe of all political progressives, comes in for its share of lumps. The "new politics," he tells us in his revolutionary voice, will be "scientific and constructive, forward looking rather than traditional, authoritative, and retrospective." But then to soothe more historical, conservative commitments, he continues, "This is not to say that the precious experience of the race will be thrown away, but to indicate that there is a wide difference between history as the artistic embalming of tradition and as the scientific knowledge of the past evolution of the race, considered with reference to the conscious direction of future evolution."

The chapter entitled "Recent History of Political Thinking" pays due respect to the traditional pantheon of theorists; but the title contains the clue. It is not "Political Thought," as it was in his book in 1903, or "Political Ideas," as it was in 1920, or "Political Theories," as recently as 1924, but "Political Thinking." Merriam's orientation

toward process had reached its conclusion; and in
a sweeping historical frame, he divides the history
of political thinking into four periods:

1. The a priori and deductive method, down
   to 1850;
2. The historical and comparative method,
   1850–1900;
3. The present tendency toward observation,
   survey, measurement, 1900–;
4. The beginnings of the psychological treatment of politics.

The relationship of stages is unclear. He was
himself, as he continued to be, a respecter and user
of the historical and comparative method, while
critics would find relationships between many of
his published statements and the a priori and deductive method, particularly where concepts like
democracy were concerned. Nor does it seem likely
that he expected the uses of observation, survey,
and measurement to become outmoded once psychology came to maturity as a method. Or did he?
It seems clearer at some times than at others that
stage three is intended as preliminary to stage
four. And what did he mean by psychology? The
chapter "Politics and Psychology" ought to provide the answer; but it starts with Plato and Aristotle and moves to a survey of recent work which

does not indicate what the answer might be. We find not an analytic statement of what psychology is or how it will in fact relate to politics, but a genial inclusion of all efforts to find psychology, whatever it is. "Wherever we find comrades in this quest for truth—and is not the search for realities in the social field the greatest need of our day— why not welcome them and catch step without examining too closely or too long their pedigrees or their passports?"

"Politics and Numbers" returns again to Plato and Aristotle. The need for "minute inquiry patiently carried out on a small scale, . . . microscopic studies of the political process carried on in an objective manner" is what he calls for. But again the sense of revolution is tempered by references to the continued reliability and support offered by safer, older traditions. "It is not to be assumed that the quantitative study of government will supersede analysis of other types, either now or perhaps at any time. Insight, judgment, analysis . . . will always continue to lead or to supplement statistical evidence." Theory, too, will remain useful, even necessary. "Hunches" will continue to guide initial inquiry. Nor does Merriam avoid comment on the dangers of excessive zeal. If political science disappears in "microscopic monographs, isolated, never synthesized, barren in interpretation," it will only be for a while. "It may well be that politics must lose its way before it finds itself again in the modern world of science. . . . We are more likely to err on the side of the unverified claims of prejudice, opinion, or interest than on that of over-emphasis on statistical measurement." There are no insurmountable obstacles in the race for an effective science, and nothing to fear in its intelligent application.

And so it goes throughout the collection. One glimpses the method and its dilemmas in "Politics in Relation to Inheritance and Environment." Those who have "fundamental facts in their possession and entertain different but important points of view" must be encouraged "to come together and integrate their knowledge in comprehensive scientific form. . . . " But this coming together is admittedly no easy matter, even though it is the essential of any integration with even a pretense to comprehensiveness. A "benevolent despot of science," Merriam suggests, might be able to "compel the union of all the scientific agencies centering around the welfare of the race. . . ." But such a despot (Merriam says "fortunately") does not exist in our "world of freedom." Why fortunately? But never mind and do not fear. A surrogate is offered.

"Perhaps the initiative should come from the students of government, interested as they are fundamentally in coordination and cooperation, in management and morale, in the elimination of social waste through unnecessary friction, misunderstanding, and misdirection. In a sense it may be said, therefore, that the heaviest load is that laid upon the political scientist."

It was a load which Merriam was willing enough to bear for a time and an initiative which he, as a political scientist, proved sufficient to providing. Whether he did it as a scientist pressed to investigation and research or as a politician skilled in the arts of rhetoric and the manipulation of the always hard-pressed assemblage of available resources is another matter. Indeed, the relation between politics and science in the reorganization of political science is a puzzle his writing will not resolve, even though he felt that the pieces were all present. It is possible that in political science, as in politics in a democratic society, benevolent despotism is one of the shadows cast by anyone who succeeds in pressing himself forward in the upper reaches of leadership where the many lights are strong and equally intense.

From *New Aspects of Politics* one can put together an outline of the assumptions upon which

Merriam's concept of his own leadership was built. First, and most important, was the assumed efficacy, as well as utter necessity, of voluntarism in scientific research. The cooperation which alone could be productive of true scientific advance could not be coerced. It could be argued persuasively in open forums before the community charged with the responsibility of deciding, but it could not be forced. This is essential to an understanding of Merriam's point of view, for the whole concept of the necessary conjunction of science and democracy rests on it.

Second, Merriam assumed that fundamental differences of opinion in social science are always scientifically and rationally reconcilable, that basic difference must always be the result of error. The very nature of what has come to be called "consensus" rests on this assumption, for it means that in social science, as in natural science, adequate observation and testing will always prove one of two conflicting theories to have been incorrect. Extended conflict of ideas becomes as ultimately irrational, then, as extended conflict of armed troops. Unresolved conflict, in an ideal social science state, must always trigger more research, not more conflict. If the first assumption is recognized as voluntarism, the second might be called resolutionism, the doctrine that intellectual dispute is always rationally resolvable.

Third, Merriam gave to politics a unique and superior role among the social sciences as the sole method of achieving voluntary cooperation and resolving otherwise unresolvable intellectual disputes. The basic method is alluded to—which is as close as one gets to a description of it—in the chapter "Political Prudence." It is part art and part science and it is tested, finally, not by reference to expert elites but by the mind of the community as a whole. This is a process of "whole mind," so to speak, and it is a method of its own. It is important to note in this context that in his arrangement of the periods of methodology in political research, the "present stage" of observation, survey, and measurement—the methodological interests most often associated with behaviorism in political science—is the penultimate, not the ultimate stage. They are to be followed by a psychological stage which, as Merriam writes, is only just beginning. Whether or not one can describe it, nonetheless, it is the architectonic of his method, the method which controls the other methods. This politicism, the dependence upon politics as the ultimate method, rests in part at least on his assumption that a kind of intellectual administration is the basic method of making social science useful, and that the ultimate utilization of social science is an absolute necessity which can be brought about only by the perfection of political science.

The emphasis upon the political in political science was what separated Merriam's progressivism from the progressive tradition in social science as well as in politics. Politics had been one of the primary targets of progressive marksmen ever since the days of the Tammany tiger hunt. Politicians were fair game for every kind of reformer, and the season never closed. By the 1920s the term politics conjured up an image of sham and dishonesty intended to leave no doubt that the mere taint was sufficient to discredit any otherwise sensible undertaking or point of view. "Getting the politics out" was the initial step in the modernization of any system or the sanitizing of any issue. In more sophisticated circles, nationally and internationally, the purpose of social science and social revolution alike was to make politics, as it had been known in western society for almost two centuries, unnecessary.

In his presidential address to the American Political Science Association in 1925 Merriam commented wryly on the tendency among his social science colleagues to use the phrase "Well, of course, that is purely political" to express "the absolute absence of science in any subject." And he went on to say, "We are even solemnly warned that politics is disappearing. I have read with great interest the comments of those who seem to believe that we are about to pass into a world from which the wicked spirit of politics has been exorcised, into a depoliticized, denatured state—no, not state but status—in which nonpolitical rule has taken the place of the outlawed scapegoat once called politics. It is easy to understand what these writers feel and sometimes even what they mean, but I am unable to share their convictions, and it is difficult to escape the conclusion that they are deceiving themselves with euphonious verbalisms. Whether the ruling authority is called economic, or social, or political, or by some other name hereafter to be determined, a set of relations similar to those of politics seems to be inevitable."

If the inevitability of politics as a continuing force in human behavior separated Merriam from one central strand of the progressive tradition, his faith in the necessary public utility of social science would remain as the sign of the deeper, unbreakable bond. Social theory, whatever its claim to purity and abstraction, could not assert its claim to science until it returned for testing to the empirical ground from which it had sprung. The ultimate return to experience was thus not only the beginning point of all social research, it was as well the end point of all social practice, the necessary enriching of the empirical ground out of which new research would come. That this cyclical process was voluntary, at the same time that it produced the clarity and certitude of science, was what necessitated the dependence upon the kind of social politics which Merriam summed up in the term prudence.

Merriam's presidential address to the association marked the twenty-first anniversary of the separation of political science from history, an event which Merriam had aided and abetted from the beginning. His statement was a plea for a new maturity which would match that symbolic majority, a new responsibility to be built upon verification rather than the "complacent philosophical gestures conjuring new worlds from airy hypotheses" of men like Plato and Comte. He called for "a freer spirit, a forward outlook, an emancipation from clinging categories now outgrown, a greater creativeness in technique, a quicker fertility of investigation, a more intimate touch with life, a balanced judgment, a more intense attack upon our problems, closer relations with other social sciences and with the natural sciences—with these we may go on to the reconstruction of the 'purely political' into a more intelligent influence on the progress of the race toward conscious control over its own evolution."

These words would be parodied and attacked the next year from the same platform by Charles Beard in his presidential address. The display of professional anger would hurt Merriam deeply, although the two men, both products of the same period of the Burgess and Dunning influence at Columbia, had never been more than distantly friendly rivals. Some listeners would be shocked, some pleased, none neutral. The dispute was profound and considerably more real than the metaphors in which it was couched; but it was without direct effect on Merriam's leadership in the profession. Whatever the intellectual bases of that ineffectiveness—and they are worth exploring in other contexts—Merriam had decided to exert control over the institutions of support for the kind of research he was exhorting the profession to undertake. Those institutions, the universities and philanthropic foundations, were the institutions from which Beard, in an equally deliberate decision, had virtually separated himself.

The last paragraph of Merriam's address was,

in effect, a blueprint for the next fifteen years of his life, although in the light of what he seemed to be doing at the time, it has a peculiar foreboding to it, the quality not of a beginning but of a farewell. He called upon the new generation of political scientists to "take over an unfinished work," acknowledging that "fundamental readjustment is the problem of another and younger generation." And he concluded, "we rely confidently on their insight, technique, judgment, and vision to effect the more perfect development of a science on which we labored long but left so much to do." Merriam was well aware of the fact that the promised land of scientific revolution was yet a long way off, although he was convinced that he had had the vision of it. He was aware, too, that his students and their students stood a much better chance of actually living in that world than he and his contemporaries ever could have. He recognized, too, the pains of adjustment, because he suffered from them himself.

In the five years from 1920 to 1925, then, Merriam had succeeded in constructing for himself an approach to political science which would characterize the rest of his career, although the elements of that approach provide a number of interesting questions concerning the evolution of a modern discipline. The addition of "The Present State of the Study of Politics" and the presidential address, "Progress in Political Research," to *New Aspects of Politics* provides as complete a doctrinal canon and litany for those years as one can assemble, although the basic methods involved may be as dependent upon what those writings represent as upon what they actually say. For in a sense they constitute only part of the method Merriam used to influence and restructure his profession.

Any forebodings he may have had about the decline of his career after 1925 were wasted, although critics of his writings who looked in his books for the research he pressed upon others were not inclined to think so. From 1925 until his retirement in 1940 his influence in the profession increased in precisely the fashion his presidential address predicted: in the sending into the profession of men and women committed to finding the hard realities which underlay his dreams. But that influence was by no means built upon dreams. Merriam's influence rested upon three elements which he juggled with considerable skill: exhortation, organization, and money. These writings represent the hortatory phase of his work. His influence at the University of Chicago—both in and out of its Department of Political Science—in the

American Political Science Association, the Social
Science Research Council, philanthropic foundations, and the federal government represent the
other two. In many important respects, his power
over any one of the three would have come to
nought without the cooperation of the others. At
the same time, from the point of view of the social
science revolution he sought to influence, his writing may have looked dated—even disappointing—
as it had begun to look before the end of his life.
That he was not the social scientist his students became may still say more about his success in ac-
complishing exactly what he wanted to accomplish
—a revolution in the profession—than it does about
any supposed failure as a political scientist. A
critical search among his writings for the methodological refinements and adventures in technical
elegance he seemed to demand from others would
be the kind of exercise in futility which all of his
best students quickly learned to avoid. What they
and others wanted from him was something entirely different; and for a remarkable number of
years—by today's rapidly shifting standards—
there is no doubt that they got it.

Contemporaries who criticized Merriam's lack
of concern with "real" scientific method (men like
Robert T. Crane and William F. Ogburn) or excess

of concern with scientific method (Charles Beard) were also quite capable of criticizing one another even more severely than they needed to criticize Merriam. Indeed, throughout the reports of meetings like the National Conference on the Science of Politics and the many other efforts at cooperation during the period are undercurrents of serious doctrinal dispute sufficient to tax the talents of the most nimble conference reporter. Thurstone's attempt to report Merriam's discussion of political prudence at a round table on psychology is a case in point. The difficulty is scarcely concealed. Merriam saw the differences clearly enough; but his demand for the continuity of constructive communication stemmed always from his repeated insistence that they were all too far from any central, confirmable truths to be able to justify a level of internecine conflict which even threatened in its intensity to limit communication.

The resulting "pluralism," as Merriam often put it, could be decried by those in search of rigor and definition. It could be attributed to a fascination with novelty—which it often was—but it was more than that. It was also a concerted effort to maintain openness at a moment in time when disciplinary specialization threatened to narrow the utility of the social sciences in the search for precision. For the human being was a whole cultural being who could be studied through a microscope but not necessarily enabled thereby to live as a citizen of a good society. Even with the then distant possibility of genetic manipulation before him, Merriam still rested his case for democracy on the ultimate survival of his cooperative pluralism. Such an approach, often mislabeled pragmatic by those who wanted to see a Franklinesque kite-flying in the supposed social experimentalism of New Deal crisis planning, generated conflict over which a skillful rhetoric was forced to cast the illusion of resolution.

The fact was, moreover, that Merriam's generation of new social scientists not only could not justify too intense a level of inter- or intra-disciplinary conflict, they could not (in very pragmatic terms) afford it. Foundation directors, businessmen reformers, high government officials—even presidents—and members of Congress seeking expert justification for approving appropriations were not as interested in debates which revealed doubts and indecisions, let alone sharp professional disagreements, as they were in programs which promised the assurance of scientific efficacy and technological efficiency. To justify the public expense—and what many assumed to be the risks—of public application of theories of experimental social research, that research would have to be buttressed by claims of competence which supported costs and soothed apprehension. Open conflict among experts was not likely to generate such an atmosphere. If Merriam knew the parable of the blind Indians who defined the elephant with reference to the parts of it their hands could feel, he saw the necessary concluding step as a rational conference in which the experts would pool their separate experiences to produce a reasonable account of a whole animal, not as a battle to the death over which one had experienced the truth. Rationality could transcend blindness, and confidence in that rationality, eloquently displayed, could sell social science to those who needed it the most. Merriam's emphasis, therefore, was on the promise of the shared community of intellectuals.

The method did produce the community Merriam sought, though that aspect of it—the necessity of continuous, supportive cooperation—was perhaps its most elusive. From 1925 to 1940 Merriam succeeded in pressing his method on a large part of the social science research which Americans were engaged in; but by the end of the period even his beloved Chicago department had begun to slip from his grasp, and he considered at one point trying to replace the Social Science Research Council with a new group committed to reinvigorating his cooperative dream. But his energy and his power were gone. It had been a mighty effort, useful and necessary in its time, though bought at a price he could not have envisaged.

Part of that utility and part of that price can be seen in the writings collected here. The forming of a national academic profession devoted to national reform shared problems with a national politics or party system. There was no tradition of a Royal Society centralized enough to make despotic rule effective, even had ideology permitted it—as in Merriam's case it explicitly did not. As a result, the level of generality which would attract the maximum number of adherents with a minimum amount of offense to any group could come dangerously close to contradiction and inconsistency when applied to intellectual matters like scientific method. Thus, we are told a number of things which anyone who has observed the development of the disciplines since 1940 might view with a kind of bemused skepticism, if not out-and-out pain. Quantification and measurement ought not endanger traditional interest in political theory. The security of Plato and Aristotle will remain a base from which to move. We can depend on our advice from Machiavelli and Hobbes, once we have modernized them sufficiently. History and the new politics are really compatible. No one need feel threatened by change. It is all very new and revolutionary, but very safe and secure. There is a place for everyone on the bench of the converted— but first they must be converted. The only question is "to what?" and the answer is deceptively simple—or it was in his day. We must come to understand that the application of science to human affairs is not in itself the basic threat faced by democratic traditions. That was the optimism which lasted until World War II; but unlike Alice's experience with the Cheshire cat, it was the smile which disappeared first.

Nonetheless, to use such generalities and suspicions as the basis for too rigorous a criticism risks missing the point by removing the text from the historical context which gives it its fundamental meaning. The 1920s and 30s was a period bursting at the seams with half-formed, untested new ideas about the nature and role of government. Throughout Europe when the fabric of nineteenth-century liberal democracy seemed to be yielding under the weight of World War I and the social and economic reverberations it set in motion, the programs which fought to replace that fabric were at first sufficiently backed with a sense of revolutionary promise to merit cautious support at the very least. But then Mussolini's Fascism became Hitler's; Lenin's Russia became Stalin's; and the experiments could no longer be observed from a respectful if somewhat suspicious distance. Whether the emergence of tyranny was a logical evolution of the social theories themselves was a question too dramatically caught up in the seemingly inevitable rush of events to remain relevant. American scholars had read Weber and Michels, and they were reading one another. But they were watching a world once again headed for war, and there was less and less room for the subtleties of calm, uncommitted observation.

Throughout the 1920s what they had found in their own approaches to government was not the systematic application of science to political life which they both admired and feared in what they saw of European social and governmental approaches to reform but a cacaphonous Babel of conflicting promises still bathed in the rhetoric of progressivism. And even that security was under persistent threat, as Merriam's references to the Scopes trial and the more sophisticated examples of repressive educational legislation in the 1920s indicates. The New Deal promised them their reforms but denied them their commitment to system, so they once again refurbished pragmatism as a concept and worshipped a magical Roosevelt who shared their dreams but violated their methods. For those concerned with the implications of social theory for the maintenance of social order and the continuity of social values, it was not an easy time. Prosperity had provided the popular trappings of an affluence which either ignored or threatened democratic traditions by concealing the unprosperous from general view. Depression could only exacerbate the emerging sense of disorder. Intellectually, as well as economically, the United States was rich in resources, but resources so seriously maldistributed that the paradox of rotting crops and starving peoples loomed as a threat paralleled by the availability of useful ideas insufficiently known by those who needed to know them and insufficiently tested in public experiment to render them worse than useless. The problem could be focused on organization and distribution, not on originality or innovation. But there was also the problem of confidence, of sustaining the assurance that what was new and useful was not dangerous. Franklin Roosevelt was not alone in his awareness of the threat posed by unreasoning fear. His own unreasoning confidence in the validity of plural

experimentalism papered over paradox and contradiction, emphasizing the utility of conflict rather
than its cost. Merriam's approach to the community of social scientists was similar in its emphasis
upon a pluralism in which a higher order as yet
unperceived in most of its parts would bring har-
mony to all diligent efforts in the search for science.

New Aspects of Politics can be used to cast
light on some important elements of post–World
War I progressivism and reform, its confidence and
optimism, its links with earlier progressivism, its
emphasis upon organization and distribution, its
dependence upon a kind of rhetoric which sees
consensus in chaos and searches for the productive
aspects of conflict. It can also serve to indicate the
roots of the reaction which followed World War II.
Like all effective prophecy, it enriched its promises with metaphor and breadth, straining to see in
the confusion of a vision some comfort for everyone. Like all effective prophecy, perhaps, the price
of its power in its day may be the measure of the
disillusion it came to provoke. As Merriam seemed
to know, and as *New Aspects of Politics* may demonstrate, the social science of a society committed
to democratic methods of reform rests on a delicate
balance between prophecy and precision. The necessary search for public support may precede the

scientific certitude which the support presumes. The right to experiment must be built on persuasion, not on force. It is a process filled with intellectual danger and desperately dependent upon intellectual responsibility. The relation between the two may hold the key to whatever understanding any generation achieves of its intellectual origins and whatever hope it has for the possibility of a future.

Preface to the Second Edition

In another five years I shall perhaps be able to prepare a different treatise on the still newer aspects of politics, but I am not ready to do so now, and, in view of my mental unpreparedness, have compromised by writing a supplementary preface to the present volume. In this I am endeavoring to point out some of the more striking tendencies in political research since the publication of the first edition, in 1925. They are not, I may hasten to say, consequences of my little book, but concomitants—joint evidence of the deep unrest that pervades the world of social and political science.

Most important of all the changes since 1925 is the greatly quickened interest in the social sciences, not alone in the United States but also in many nations of Western Europe and even in the Orient. This has found expression on the formal side in the establishment of the Social Science Research Council of the United States,[1] of many minor councils in different universities, and of the rise of numerous

[1] See annual reports of this Council; also proceedings of the annual conferences at Dartmouth, New Hampshire; particularly the discussion in 1928 on the trends of social research and the New Program adopted in 1929.

institutions for generalized or special social research, both in the United States and in various European countries—a list so long that the enumeration of names would prove tiresome.

The trends of this awakening interest in the social sciences take the form of a broader view of the interrelations of the several social disciplines,[1] of numerous attempts at co-operative research on the part of various hitherto overdepartmentalized groups, of sharper analysis of methods of inquiry, of an effort to reach greater objectivity in approach, and of stronger emphasis on realism in material.[2]

There is also evident a disposition on the part of the social scientists to bridge the gap between social research and the domain of biological research, including under the biological the medical and the fringes of psychiatry and psychoanalysis. Research in such fields as personality and child development

[1] See Ogburn and Goldenweiser, *The Social Sciences*; E. C. Hayes, *Social Sciences*; and *Methods in Social Science: A Casebook*, edited by Stuart Rice, which represents a beginning in the study of methodology, although far from a satisfactory solution.

[2] *The New Social Science*, containing addresses delivered on the occasion of the dedication of the Social Science Research Building at the University of Chicago, provides much pertinent material on this subject. See also *Chicago, an Experiment in Social Science Research*, for description of a local experiment.

are illustrative of the undertakings of this type. Although no adequate survey has been made of the personal and institutional developments of this character in Europe and America, it is clear that a notable movement in this direction is well under way. This approach points toward a comprehensive and intensive study of human behavior, focusing upon it all the techniques and skills of the social and the biological sciences. A quiet revolution is going on, the results of which are likely to be far more eventful for mankind than the noisier and more dramatic social and political demonstrations that have occupied, the attention of the race.

In view of this rapid growth of interest in the social sciences, it may be assumed that the future development of the study of government will proceed on a far more fundamental basis than has hitherto been the case and that the possibilities of scientific advance will be greatly enriched and enhanced. An expression of this new movement in governmental research is seen in the 1930 report of the American Political Science Association, in which the elements of a program are indicated, reflecting the new stream of tendencies, social and economic, and indicating new directions and new methods.[1] A perusal of this document will supply

[1] *American Political Science Review*, February, 1930, pp. 25–69.

ample evidence of the richer possibilities in the study of government, unfolded by the events and trends of recent years.[1] It is not without significance in this connection, that the original recommendation for the establishment of closer relations among the social sciences and for the establishment of a Council for this purpose was made by the research committee of the Political Science Association.

Another striking development of the period has been the emergence of judicial research at a number of centers in the United States. In Harvard, Columbia, Yale, the traditional vocational law schools have been supplemented by agencies for the promotion of research in the basic problems of law; while in Johns Hopkins a juristic institute has sprung up without a vocational background. Especial attention has been given to the discovery of the social and economic bases and interrelations of law,[2] and its relations with psychology, psychiatry, and medicine, to its methodology even. This tendency has been earlier observable in Continental jurisprudence, and had long been forecast here by

[1] See also previous reports of the three conferences on the science of government in the *American Political Science Review*, 1923–25.

[2] See Johns Hopkins University publication, *Current Research in Law*, for a summary of these tendencies.

Roscoe Pound, but only within the last few years has it found root in the soil of American legal study and begun to bud and blossom. The direction and speed of this movement cannot be predicted; and, indeed, its chief significance lies in the clear and unmistakable indication that the important field of formal law will not be omitted from the searching study of human behavior now under way.

Since 1925 there have been important developments in the study of the political process, some of which may be sketched here. Increasing interest in the application of measurement to political phenomena has been evident within the past few years. Notable among these studies are the works of Gosnell,[1] Rice,[2] Catlin,[3] Allport,[4] Giese,[5] White,[6] Thurstone,[7] and Florence.[8] The important consid-

[1] *Getting Out the Vote* and *Why Europe Votes.*

[2] *Quantitative Methods in Politics.*

[3] *Science and Method in Politics; Principles of Politics.*

[4] "Measurement and Motivation of a Typical Opinion in a Certain Group," *American Political Science Review*, XIX (1925), 735–60; "A Technique for the Measurement and Analysis of Public Opinion," *Proceedings of the American Sociological Society*, XX (1926), 241–44.

[5] *Die öffentliche Persönlichkeit.*

[6] L. D. White, *Prestige Value of Public Employment in Chicago.*

[7] L. L. Thurstone: (with Chave) *The Measurement of Attitude* (1929); and numerous articles.

[8] P. S. Florence, *The Statistical Method in Economics and Political Science.*

eration here is not the results achieved but the direction and method of the inquiry, which is for the moment more important than the goal attained by the particular investigation. The attempt to find measurable units of political phenomena is of very great interest to the student of political science, even though the particular methods and results may be crude and unsatisfactory in many respects.

A type of experiment was that conducted by Mr. Gosnell and published under the title *Getting Out the Vote.* This was an effort to measure the effect of certain stimuli upon voters of various types and classes in a particular election, using a control group and an experimental group. But in general, scholars still stand mute before the task either of setting up experiments in this field or of intensive and accurate observation of experiments actually going on. It may safely be predicted, however, that another generation will see important advances in this sector.

Progress has been made in the direction of studies on the borderline between politics and psychology or psychiatry. Conspicuous here is Lasswell's *Psychopathology and Politics,* a daring and original adventure in the study of political personality from the point of view of psychoanalysis,

UNIVERSITY OF WINNIPEG
LIBRARY
515 _____ Avenue
Winnipeg, Man. ____ 2B 2E9

DISCARDED

almost the first of its kind. Of very great value also
are the notable studies of Thurstone and Allport in
the measurement of opinion, and the development
of scales for this purpose.[1] Kretschmer's *Physique
and Character* is a study of great importance with
reference to the relation between types of physical
constitution and political behavior.[2]

It will be some time before the smoke has cleared
away from even the first battles in the field of
physiology, constitutionalism, psychology, psychiatry, psychoanalysis, social science, and their
various combinations and permutations. But we
may reasonably anticipate a much clearer view of
the human "personality," or whatever the axis or
axes of this problem may be called in the next stage
of inquiry. The implications of this development
for the study of the political personality, and for
the understanding of the process and the modes of
control over social and political behavior, are very
numerous and important and may well have a determining influence on the trends and methods of

[1] See *supra*.

[2] Compare E. Miller, *Types of Mind and Body*. A useful summary
of modes of approach is given in Thomas' *Child in America*; also in
A. A. Roback's *Psychology of Character*. Other studies of interest in
this field are Lange-Eichbaum, *Genie-Irrsinn und Ruhm* (1928), and
H. S. Sullivan, *Personal Psychopathology*. Other titles are conveniently
cited in Lasswell, *op. cit.*, Appendix A.

political science. Difficult as the task may be, the integration of social and biological data with political data is of prime importance in the long look forward; and those who neglect this field will be in danger of finding themselves surviving in political antiquarianism and mythology.

A dissenting opinion on the newer types of political research has been filed by Laski,[1] who protests against co-operative research and against the realistic forms of investigation, sometimes characterized as "field work," at least to the extent that they interfere with the "lonely thinker" and with appropriate diet of principles. Likewise, Charles A. Beard is concerned lest the study of politics lay too great stress upon the scientific aspects of inquiry and too little upon humanistic implications of social research.[2] But it would be unfair to conclude that either of these writers wishes to do more than file a caveat regarding undue emphasis on methodology as against creative intelligence, and materials to the exclusion of values.

Nor have there been wanting contributions to systematic political theory during these last years. Kelsen's *Allgemeine Staatslehre* is a notable contribution to this domain of inquiry by a pupil of

[1] *The Dangers of Disobedience*, chap. vi.

[2] See University of Virginia publications on social research.

Jellinek. Laski's *Grammar of Politics* continues the
tradition of English political speculation, interpreted now by a left-wing Laborite. Catlin's *Principles
of Politics* does not, strictly speaking, belong in this
group, although sections of it might be allocated
there. Dewey has continued the application of
pragmatism to social and political problems, notably in his *Public and Its Problems*, and Smith in his
Democratic Way of Life.[1] Italian, Russian, and Indian philosophers have stated their respective doctrines in impressive form, particularly in the writing of Gandhi and of Rocco.

It can by no means be said that the road to progress in this direction is blocked; but further advance may depend upon a new statement of rationalism or of pragmatism, as the case may be, in
terms more nearly adapted to the problems of research in the field of social and political phenomena. It may reasonably be expected that a new synthetic philosophy will emerge, fusing the materials
now found scattered throughout the natural sciences, the social sciences, and the humanities, into
a new interpretation with perhaps a new logic.
But "science" will be inside, not outside, this new
philosophy when it appears. The whole structure

[1] Compare Elliot's *Pragmatic Revolt in Politics* (1928), a trenchant
critique of Laski.

42 of the modern political order imperatively demands re-examination of its fundamentals in the
light of modern economic and social conditions, of
modern technology, the new morality, the new
science, the new philosophy. Here the adventurous
political theorist may find full sweep for his analytical and synthetic faculties, weaving together
the new data developed by modern research.

Fruitful lines of inquiry starting with the approach of the anthropologist have been indicated by
Rivers in his *Psychology and Politics*, and by Myres
in his *Influence of Anthropology upon Political Science;* but these have not thus far been closely
followed up. The studies of Lowie and others indicate, however, some of the possibilities in this general direction,[1] and it seems probable that in the
near future some enterprising scholars will undertake to combine the points of view of politics and
anthropology in a new synthesis of interpretation.
A suggestive study of this type is Weber's *Duk-
Duks*—an examination of primitive methods of ini-
tiation into group life, not confined, however, to
primitives alone. It is quite clear that for the further development of anthropology the more intensive view of the student of government and of
economics will be necessary for the interpretation

[1] *Origin of the State.*

of the life of the special groups upon which the anthropologist concentrates. And out of this situation there may well develop relations of great value both to anthropology and government.

The opportunities for the reconstruction of the science of politics are found on every hand. Political theory, never as sterile as it may momentarily seem, awaits new syntheses, new interpretations, perhaps a new logic. Public administration is at the brink of much more scientific treatment in which the newer techniques in the study of human personality will be utilized and in which the common problems of administration running through a series of social groups will be recognized. International relations is ready for the touch of those who can add to the juristic and historical methods the quickening spirit of modern economic and social science and revolutionize now antiquated modes of study. Party phenomena invite a keener analysis in which the nature of public opinion, of pressure groups, of propaganda, will be found of fundamental importance. Students of legislation are confronted by unparalleled opportunities for the investigation of quasi-parliamentary types of social control in a pluralistic world. Those who are interested in political personality and in leadership find abundant and increasing material in the more

44   general studies of social science and its fringes in biology and medicine. Nationalism, urbanism, and other types of loyalties are of challenging importance and now may be approached by intensive and objective methods impossible a generation ago. Public law, on the border between politics and jurisprudence, is almost certain to be transformed in the process by which the study of jurisprudence is now being revolutionized; and the student of government is indispensable in this process. Civic training, in its framework of social training, presents a practical problem of the very first magnitude, and a scientific process in which many modern devices may be employed with very great advantage. Viewing the field of political research, we seem indeed to be entering an era of notable change in methods and materials—a period of unusual opportunity for scientific adventure of the most fruitful type.

A striking feature of the last few years has been the increasing employment of technical information and advice in the formulation of governmental plans of action. One outstanding example of this tendency is seen in the extraordinary development of the technical aids to government in the League of Nations' secretariat at Geneva, particularly in their application to public health, but almost equally evident in many other branches of the service. Another is the appointment by President Hoover of a committee of experts to report upon recent social trends as a basis for the formation of a forward-looking national policy. This had been preceded by a similar report on recent economic changes. In England, France, Russia, and other states wide use has been made of expert advice in recent political and economic crises, and in dealing with complex social situations.

Likewise, there have been imposing advances in the organization of public officials for the interchange of information and experience and for the projection of new plans of action. Conspicuous among these is the German Städtetag, with its remarkable facilities for the prompt collection and exchange of municipal experiences. The International Union of Cities is a like enterprise on a large scale, and many smaller organizations are springing up at widely scattered points in response to the same common impulse for the better interchange of governmental experiences in the conduct of somewhat similar experiments. The recently organized Public Administration Clearing House in the United States is an example of the same conspicuous trend toward more effective organization of political experience. The efficiency or rationalization movement has given new impetus to these movements in many instances, partly because of the pressure of taxes and partly because of the analogy with large-scale methods of production. It is on the whole likely that very substantial progress will be made at this point in the immediate future. The close observation of governmental experiments, the prompt interchange of experience, the thoughtful consideration of the data assembled, will go far toward the wise management of public affairs. If government does not become more scientific, it will at least rest on a higher type of political prudence.

Summing up the tendencies evident during the last few years, we find an impressive development of interest and activity in social science, a freer interpenetration of the several branches of social research, a tendency toward bridging the gap between social science and the biological and medical sciences and toward building an integrated study of human behavior, increasing attention to the material and method of political science and to the mechanisms for the prosecution of research. Still more specific trends are those in the direction of quantification, toward study of the physical and psychiatric aspects of political personality and be-

havior, toward more realistic study of such devices
as propaganda, the ways of pressure groups, the
new forms of industrio-political organization, the
inevitable and symptomatic protest against over-
mechanization and methodological emphasis, and
finally the faint signs of a revival of interest in the
logic and philosophy of politics. On the practical
side there has been evident a powerful trend toward more effective organization and exchange of
the information and experience of governing officials and research groups generally.

There are many indications that out of these
new situations there will arise conditions more favorable to creative political thought, more con-
ducive to the attainment of a higher level in political observation, experiment and speculation alike.
Political maladjustments of the most formidable
and menacing type threaten modern civilization at
various points, and he would be a rash prophet who
should promise the speedy and certain cure of all
the ills the body politic is heir to. There are signs
of still greater cataclysms than those the race has
yet experienced in the economic, the political, the
moral order. Mankind may writhe in sharper an-
guish and in darker despair than ever. But there
are also signs (and temperament perhaps deter-

48   mines which view one takes) of the emergence of a higher type of political and social science through which human behavior may be more finely adjusted and its deeper values more perfectly unfolded, as the art and science of human living progressively develop their fuller possibilities.

CHARLES E. MERRIAM

JANUARY 2, 1931

Preface to the First Edition

It has become commonplace to say that we are living in a world of rapidly changing social relations. The ways that were adequate one hundred years ago are in many particulars no longer adapted to many phases of human life, and notable adjustments are everywhere being made. But of equal or greater significance than social changes is the swift reorganization of intellectual equipment and methods, now in process of revolutionizing the world. In this situation we may ask, What place has politics in the new world of social and mental organization? In what manner can politics and modern science go along together? Will politics tend to disappear altogether from the scene, or to persist as an indispensable nuisance, or will it take on some of the characteristics we now call scientific?

One answer to the challenge of the new time is that the age has come for the "passing of politics." We must, it is said, "depoliticize" social affairs, turn our backs on state and government, boycott politics, and endeavor to reconstruct new types of institutions other than those we now call political.

This protest, however, is no new phenomenon

50 in history. Nor will it stand the test of analysis. There have always been anarchists and antistateists of various types since the dawn of organized political society. Not only because "no rogue e'er felt the halter draw with good opinion of the law," but because various interests, individual or group, have felt themselves unjustly treated by the state and have rationalized their grievances into arguments not merely against the government that oppresses them, but against all states at all times.

But would there be any magic in the change of name that would essentially alter the process of political control? The balance of social and industrial groups may be and has been changed, but would "a democratic supreme court of functional equity," as suggested by Mr. G. D. H. Cole, be very much different from the government with its co-ordinating function today? The difficulty is that altering the name of what has been called "politics" will not change the operations that have hitherto been characterized by that term. The processes will go on under some other title.

The real answer to this challenge of politics is the consideration and adoption of more scientific and intelligent methods in the study and practice of government. We may ask how, in the new world in which we live, the new politics may be most effectively developed. Both in theory and in practice, how may political science make best use of all that the other sciences are contributing to modern thought and practice?

The objectives of politics may be briefly summarized from one point of view as:

I. The elimination of waste in political action.

II. The release of political possibilities in human nature.

I. Among the greatest wastes which politics might avoid or minimize are the following:

1. War

2. Revolutions (civil wars)

3. Imperfect adjustment of individuals and classes

Typical situations causing enormous losses are the following:

1. Graft

2. Spoils

3. Exploitation

4. Inaction arising from inability to overcome inertia and deadlock

5. Instability arising from lack of equilibrium of groups

6. Clash between science and authority leading to disregard of and failure to assimilate quickly the results of modern science

All of these lead to lowered productivity and lowered good feeling, each of which affects the other in making up the sum of human well-being.

II. The second great task of politics is that of releasing the constructive possibilities in human political nature. Historically government has served a useful purpose, but has used largely agencies that now tend to be outworn, such as force; fear; routine; magic, mumbo-jumbo, prestige; selfish group interest. There are other larger possibilities, however, in the organization of human intelligence, in appreciation of the needs of social and political organization, in scientific adjustments of individuals and groups through the agencies of education, eugenics, psychology, biology. Modern methods of government would unlock the constructive faculties of human nature and make possible impressive achievements. Generally speaking, in education and in organization we have long since ceased to rely on force, fear, magic, or routine, and in proportion as we have been able to replace these factors by scientific analysis and reorganization, progress has been made. Politics is now groping its way in the dark, but must learn the use of the agencies of modern civilization for its tasks.

It is not to be presumed that in the near future

any system of political science can prevent war, revolution and imperfect adjustment, but the shock of these conflicts may gradually be minimized. Probably war can be prevented, revolutions reduced to remote possibilities, and maladjustments vastly reduced in number and intensity. At any rate, these are the tasks and these are the tests of scientific politics.

Historically the contrivances of politics are not negligible, although they may now seem somewhat commonplace. Among them are the state, the courts, representative parliamentary process, public administration, with their crude rules of justice and rough laws for burden-bearing and public order. But on the whole they were immense advances from the régime of tooth and claw which they superseded. The oral dialectic of the court may seem to work hardship in many cases, the conference and compromise of parliamentary bodies may seem timid and slow and inadequate, the rules may be outworn and hard pressed by modern needs; but on the whole these contrivances are milestones in the evolution of the race, and they constitute advances fundamental to the growth of civilization with its industrial and cultural institutions.

The political process has been made up of two elements, loyal adherence to tradition, and rest-

54 less contrivance and invention looking to change and adaptation. In politics as in life, dubious contrivances are first contested, then adopted, then made automatic; and then we go on to new situations. The new rule of the road is hard to learn, it is resisted, but it becomes automatic—and is itself the basis of resistance to some newer rule of the road evolved from some new condition.

This implies a process of readjustment, a constant readaptation to changing conditions. Sometimes this has been brought about in the throes of revolution, and sometimes by more peaceful but slower methods. It has always been one of the great tasks of politics, perhaps its greatest, to make the shocks of change as short and as little wasteful as possible. The law, the court, the police, the bureaucracy, the parliamentarian, the diplomat, the treaty, the league have all been useful for the purpose of releasing social energy that might otherwise have gone into personal and national brawls.

That the mechanisms and the means of politics have sometimes been perverted, so that social disservice has been rendered rather than service, is not surprising. The military establishment may advance beyond group protection to aggressive war, the court may be an instrument of injustice, the parliament may cloak corrupt designs of in-

triguers, the administration may become an ineffi-
cient bureaucracy. But this is no more true of the
state than of the church or of other social and economic institutions, whose organizations may become ends in themselves rather than means to an
end. All these institutions have their parasites,
their perverters, their traitors, their fussy incom-
petents who use the symbolism of the church or
the chamber of commerce or the labor union or the
university for wholly inappropriate purposes. And
the same thing may be said of any human institution.

Have we not reached the time when it is necessary to adjust and adapt more intelligently, to apply the categories of science to the vastly important
forces of social and political control? We compla-
cently assume that all will always be well, but at
any time out of depths of ignorance and hatred
may emerge world-war, anarchy, industrial and
political revolution, recurring discontent and dis-
tress. What advantage shall we reap if science
conquers the whole world except the world's government, and then turns its titanic forces over to a
government of ignorance and prejudice, with laboratory science in the hands of jungle governors?

This readjustment is one of the most urgent
tasks of our time, and one which if not successfully

carried through may result in the wreck of modern civilization. A distinguished physicist said to me not long ago, "It might be best if all physical research were stopped for a time in order that the social sciences may catch up." This is not necessary; but it is important—more than important, urgent—that the methods of social science and of political science be thoroughly scrutinized and that they be adapted to the new time in which we live and the remarkable physical world into which we are swiftly coming.

In the evolution of science it may well be that exact knowledge of human relations comes last, waiting for the development of seemingly less intricate relations. But that, if true, would not constitute an adequate reason for lagging too far in the rear. It will not do to make the thing we characterize as "human nature" the scapegoat for our own sins of inertia or unintelligence. Indeed, it has not been demonstrated that political behavior is any more complex than that of the atom, once regarded as simple and basic, but now appearing to be a miniature cosmos in itself.

Obviously this readjustment is not the task of any one individual, or even of any set of individuals, for the new methods will be worked out in actual experience and through experiment running over a period of years. It is not the purpose of this study, accordingly, to develop a new method, but to suggest certain possibilities of approach to a method, in the hope that others may take up the task and through reflection and experiment eventually introduce more intelligent and scientific technique into the study and practice of government, and into popular attitudes toward the governing process.

A word regarding the related social sciences may not be inappropriate. Trained in the historical and comparative method, "sitting at the feet of Gamaliel" in Columbia University and later in the University of Berlin, I am not unmindful of the significance of the study of the history of human experience; nor, trained in public law, am I unmindful of the value of the juristic approach to the problems of political theory and practice. That economics and sociology have contributed lavishly to the development of politics and government I should be the first to insist. In suggesting that politics sit around the table with psychology and statistics and biology and geography, I am not suggesting that we ask our older friends to go. Only this: politics must follow its problem wherever the problem leads. The rich values of history and those of jurisprudence need not and must not be lost. On the contrary, they should be treasured and applied, made integral parts of the new synthesis of knowledge which is constantly going on, not merely in politics, but in all branches of social science and of human knowledge. Drawing upon my own practical experience, I hasten to reassure some of my colleagues who seem to fear too rapid a change in the methods of political science or practice. The real danger is that our advances in method and practice will not keep up with the procession of modern thought.

It is not the purpose of this volume to suggest either a new theory of politics or a new system of government. Historically there have been many theories of the state, but these have been in large measure justifications or rationalizations of groups in power or seeking power—the special pleadings of races, religions, classes in behalf of their special situations. There will no doubt be many more of these justifications of races and classes, of Nordics and others, of proletarians, agrarians, capitalists, of Occident and of Orient. Many of these will be useful, but in the main they will not be scientific unless methods are changed under the pressure of modern intelligence. This particular study is directed toward an improvement in method of political reasoning and research rather than a form of propaganda. It is probable that there will be changes in the mechanism of government, and in any event there is certain to be prolonged discussion of the "best" form of organization, of democracy, of forms of representation, of judicial organization, and of other factors in governmental structure. Here again it must be said that the purpose of this discussion is not to suggest a specific type of organization, but rather to treat the fundamental methods of studying the political process, out of which come intelligent changes in type—in short, to make the evolution of forms more conscious and more intelligent in plan. The perfection of political education, the organization of political intelligence, the advancement of political research, and the discovery of scientific relations in the political process—these are fundamental to all theories and to all changes in form of political institutions, and these are the subject of this inquiry.

In these papers the writer has discussed the recent history of political thinking, the relation of politics to psychology, the use of the quantitative method in political inquiry, the relation of politics to the study of environment and of biology, the organization of political prudence, and other kindred topics, in the hope that others more competent might be stimulated to contribute to the new

60 politics which is to emerge in the new world: that of the conscious control of human evolution toward which intelligence steadily moves in every domain of human life.

No one appreciates more keenly than I the shortcomings of this study, both the avoidable that one stronger might have escaped, and the inevitable that arise from the nature of the present state of politics; yet I have undertaken this hazardous, or some would say hopeless, task, trusting that it might be a contribution direct or indirect to the development of clearer political thinking and sounder practice.

I am indebted to the editors of the following journals in which papers here published have appeared either in whole or in part:

The *American Political Science Review*, "The Present State of the Study of Politics," May, 1921; "Political Research," May, 1922; "Progress Report of the Committee on Political Research," May, 1923; "The Significance of Psychology for the Study of Politics," August, 1924.

The *National Municipal Review*, "The Next Step in the Organization of Municipal Research," September, 1922.

CHARLES EDWARD MERRIAM

New Aspects of Politics

1 The Present State of the Study of Politics

The original plan of this paper included a general survey and critique of the leading tendencies in the study of politics during the last thirty or forty years. It was intended to compare the methods and results of the various types of political thought—to pass in review the historical school, the juridical school, the students of comparative government, the philosophers as such, the attitude of the economist, the contributions made by the geographer and the ethnologist, the work of the statisticians, and finally to deal with the psychological, the sociological, the biological interpretations of the political process.

It would have been an interesting and perhaps a useful task to compare the scope and method of such thinkers as Jellinek, Gierke, Duguit, Dicey and Pound; the philosophies of Sorel and Dewey, of Ritchie and Russell, of Nietzsche and Tolstoi; to review of methods of Durkheim and Simmel, of Ward and Giddings and Small; of Cooley and Ross;

Reprinted with permission from *American Political Science Review* 15 (May 1921):173–85.

and to discuss the developments seen in the writings of Wallas and Cole.

It would have been useful possibly to extend the analysis to the outstanding features of the environment in which these ideas have flourished, and to their numerous and intimate relations and interrelations. It might have been possible to discuss the influence of social and industrial development, of class movements and struggles, or of group conflicts in the larger sense; to examine the influence of urbanism and industrialism; of capitalism, socialism and syndicalism; of militarism, pacificism, feminism, nationalism. It would perhaps have been useful to offer a critique of the methods and results portrayed; to make a specific appraisal of the value of the logical, the psychological, the sociological, the legal and the philosophical and the historical methodologies and their respective contributions to the study of the political.

This task was abandoned, however, and reserved for another occasion, as it became evident that no such survey could be condensed within reasonable limits. It seemed that our common purpose might be better served by a different type of analysis, aiming at the reconstruction of the methods of political study, and the attainment of larger results alike in the theoretical and the practical fields.

Within relatively recent times the theory of politics has come in contact with forces which must in time modify its procedure in a very material way. The comparatively recent doctrine that political ideas and systems—as well as other social ideas and systems—are the by-products of environment, whether this is stated in the form of economic determinism or of social environment, constitutes a challenge to all systems of thought. It can be ignored only under the penalty of losing the *locus standi* of a science. Systems may justify themselves as sounding boards of their time, but what becomes of the validity of the underlying principles usually announced with dogmatic and authoritarian emphasis?

Again, in our day the measuring scales of facts and forces have been made much finer and more exact than ever before in the history of the race. The measuring and comparing and standardizing process goes on its way, impelled by the hands of thousands of patient investigators who pursue the truth through the mazes of measurable and comparable facts. To what extent has this increased accuracy of measurement and facility in comparison of standardized observation found its way into the field of the political?

Further, on the borders of politics there have appeared in our day many allied disciplines of kindred stock. Statistics and psychology, biology, geography, ethnology and sociology have all developed and continue to produce masses of material facts, of interpretations and insights, correlations and conclusions, often bearing, directly or indirectly, upon the understanding of the political process. We may appropriately raise the question, to what extent has politics availed itself of the researches and results of these new companions in the great search for the understanding of the phenomena of human life?

Certain suggestions as to ways and means by which the technical and professional study of politics may be improved in quality and serviceability are worth some discussion. There is the question of a mechanism for the collection and classification of political material. In many ways politics has been outstripped in the race for modern equipment supplying the rapid, comprehensive and systematic assembly and analysis of pertinent facts. For business reasons the collection of certain limited classes of legal data has been systematized, and the results are promptly placed before every student of the law. For business reasons certain types of industrial data are now collected in great quantities for the use of the business man. Some of the same work is done by various bureaus of the governments. Yet in the main the political machinery is still sadly defective. The best equipped research man in the best equipped institution of learning hardly has machinery comparable with that of the best lawyer in his office, or of the best engineer, or the expert of the large corporation, or the secretary of the chamber of commerce, or the research department of the Amalgamated Clothiers. The truth is that he often has no laboratory equipment at all, and curiously enough in these days of large scale organization, he labors single-handed, even when he discusses this characteristic feature of our civilization. In this respect the political and social sciences have been generally outstripped by the so-called "natural" sciences—now often dropping the "natural"—which are far better supplied with the personnel and facilities for research.

On a larger than individual scale, there is a lack of prompt and adequate collections of great classes of laws, orders and rules. The admirable collection of the New York State Library has been discontinued and the gap never filled. The same thing is true of municipal ordinances, collections of administrative regulations, and judicial data except for reported cases. On an international scale the field is scarcely touched. It is not to be expected that political data for scientific purposes should be as quickly gathered as crop reports or legal decisions, but need the data be as scantily and infrequently reported as is now the case?

Further, the reasonably complete and prompt collection of material regarding the practical workings of political institutions is largely unorganized and only spasmodically assembled, often by propaganda agencies rather than by scientific bodies. How, for example, is material made available at present regarding the workings of the system of proportional representation, or the city manager plan of government? Chiefly by the haphazard, irregular and unsatisfactory process of observation and compilation by inadequately equipped individual workers. There is neither fund nor personnel available for extended surveys of many important fields regarding which politics should speak with some authority.

Only through the organized and persistent effort of many scholars can this defective situation be made a satisfactory one. With the cooperation of the various governmental agencies, of the several institutions of learning, and perhaps of private research funds, the workers in political science may be placed on a basis where necessary data and assistance will be available for technical use. But until then we limp where we might run.

It is not impossible that political prudence might be more effectively organized than at present. By political prudence is meant the conclusions of experience and reflection regarding the problems of the state. This constitutes a body of knowledge which, though not demonstrably and technically exact, is nevertheless a precious asset of the race. Of course it is not meant to suggest that all of this prudence is found with the professional students of politics—God forbid—but the initiative in the scientific assembly and analysis of this material may fairly be said to be one of our tasks. Certainly this falls within no other domain. It seems desirable that this mass of information, analysis, conclusion, tentative and dogmatic, accumulated by the professional students of politics should be more fully known that at present. All other groups, professional and otherwise—and there are many new ones in the last generation—express their views upon all manner of questions of state; why not the student of politics who is usually most nearly disinterested in his point of view, more comprehensive in his investigation, and impartial in his conclusions?

What is the judgment of the world's students of politics upon such problems as proportional representation, "the" or "a" League of Nations, freedom of speech under twentieth-century conditions, public ownership of public utilities—these only by way of suggestion? In many instances the counsels of professional students of politics, or of political prudence, would be divided, particularly when class, racial or nationalistic issues were raised, but in many other instances they would be united. Even their divisions would presumably rest upon at least superficially scientific grounds, and would help to turn the organization of opinion upon carefully investigated facts and careful reasoning, rather than upon group interests awkwardly disguised in ill-fitting garb. But if professional students of politics cannot come together to discuss even the fundamentals of political prudence because of the fear of violent disagreement, should not that circumstance itself cause sober reflection as to their fundamental preconceptions; and might it not suggest remodelling and reorganization of their methods? Might it not point to the weak spot in their procedure and in time lead to its strengthening?

That professional students of politics should upon all occasions and upon every transient issue rush to announce their theories and conclusions with an air of finality, is certainly not to be desired. But upon grave questions of long standing, where exhaustive inquiries have been made and all phases of a problem maturely considered, the professional opinion of special students has a certain value. Further, if students were equipped with resources for exhaustive researches through expert commissions on occasional topics, such documented inquiries and the deliberate findings based upon them might prove to be of very great use. Practical experience and observation do not lead to the conclusion that electorates or parliamentary bodies or administrative agencies are waiting breathlessly for the pronouncements of political science associations; but on the other hand the same experience and observation do suggest that they would on many occasions welcome the very sort of information, analysis and tentative conclusions of political prudence that serious professional organizations of this type could supply.

The broader the base of such a professional organization, the more effective it should be. An organization of many cities would be better than one, of many states than one, of many nations than one. For in the larger unit there is an opportunity for the elimination of the local, the class, the racial propagandas that have historically played so large a part in the formation of political theory.

Finally, the methods of politics, as of social science in general, are constantly in need of scrutiny and revision in order to avoid falling into a category that is neither scientific science nor practical politics. Of the extent to which political theory has been conscripted in the service of class and race and group we have been admirably informed by Professor Dunning. A much earlier writer says:

> In law what plea so tainted and corrupt
> But, being seasoned with a gracious voice
> Obscures the show of evil? In religion
> What damned error, but some sober brow
> Will bless it and approve it with a text,
> Hiding the grossness with fair ornament?

But that day perhaps is passing. The average man now possesses an acid test for the authoritarian doctrines which in some earlier ages he would not have been permitted to discuss, or more probably would not have thought of discussing. He begins to realize that in the excitement of racial or religious or class struggle, political theory is likely to become a pawn or piece in the larger game of military, pecuniary, or other group advantage. So it happens that we live in a time when social contrivances and control are employed more than ever before in systematic fashion, but also in a time when authority is challenged as never before. At a time when political regulation is most comprehensive, political obligation is least firmly rooted.

Sociology and social psychology offer material of the greatest value. Geography, ethnology and biology present facts and conclusions indispensable to a correct understanding of the political process, which tend to make the knowledge of that process less closely dependent upon authoritarian propaganda, and nearer the domain of scientific technology.

Statistics increase the length and breadth of the observer's range, giving him myriad eyes and making it possible to explore areas hitherto only vaguely described and charted. In a way, statistics may be said to socialize observation. It places a great piece of apparatus at the disposal of the inquirer—apparatus as important and useful to him, if properly employed, as the telescope, the microscope and the spectroscope in other fields of human investigation. But whether politics has made full use of this new instrument of inquiry may be questioned.

In the narrower sense, there are standard fields where political statistics are almost completely lacking. Notable examples in this country are our judicial and criminal statistics. In the field of operative statistics, measuring services on standardized bases, little has been done. It is a legitimate function of the political scientist to aid in the development of statistical schedules, and to ask for additional information which can be developed only in this way. In the larger sense, we have not yet surveyed the possibilities of statistical observation, and fitted it to the growth of the study of politics.

Statistics, to be sure, like logic can be made to prove anything. Yet the constant recourse to the statistical basis of argument has a restraining effect upon literary or logical exuberance, and tends distinctly toward scientific treatment and demonstrable conclusions. The practice of measurement, comparison, standardization of material—even though sometimes overdone—has the effect of sobering the discussion. We do not look forward, it is true, to a science of politics or of economics or of sociology based wholly and exclusively upon statistical methods and conclusions. We know that statistics do not contain all the elements necessary to sustain scientific life; but is it not reasonable to expect a much greater use of this elaborate instrument of social observation in the future than at present? Is it unreasonable to expect that statistics will throw much clearer light on the political and social structure and processes than we now have at our command?

Modern psychology also offers material and methods of great value to politics, and possibilities of still greater things. The statesmen and the politicians have always been psychologists by rule of thumb, and the political scientist and the economist have often tried to apply such psychology as their time afforded. The "natural" man of the *Naturrecht* school and of the classical political economy was described in the light of such information as the psychology of the day afforded. But undoubtedly Thorndike and others can tell us more about the *genus homo* than was given to Thomas Hobbes and Adam Smith. Even the psychologists— if we may accept the statements of some of them— have not always been strictly psychological in their method. The field wherein the physiologist and the behaviorist and the neurologist and the psychoanalyst and the biologist and the psycho-biologist are still busy evolving a method is a domain not yet reduced to constitutional order and government. But these new inquiries seem likely to evolve methods by which many human reactions, hitherto only roughly estimated, may be much more accurately observed, measured and compared.

They are likely to assist in the evolution of methods and means by which new relations will be discovered, new modes of adaptation contrived, and the processes of social and political control substantially modified. They are already suggesting methods by which much more accurate measurement of the human personality may be made, and much deeper insight into the social process be secured. Their work is likely to be supplemented by that of group psychology; and somewhere along the line there may by developed the study of the political personality and process, and the aspects and bearings of political psychology, which has long existed in name and in practical fact, but not in systematized form. We seem to stand on the verge of definite measurement of elusive elements in human nature hitherto evading understanding and control by scientific methods. In certain fields, such as those of education and medicine, the lines have already been thrust far out into the realm of what had always been charted as the Great Unknown. Psychology, of course, like statistics does not assume to set up the standards of social science, but is an instrument or method by which students in these fields may be materially assisted.

It is not impossible that we may have, in addition to the broad observational study of unstandardizable forces and tendencies, playing so large a part in political prudence, a more basic study of measurable and comparable political reactions, of their strength and limitations, of their possibilities of adaptation and constructive organization. This more intensive study may help to solve: (1) the problems of preliminary political education, (2) of public education in the larger sense of the term, (3) of local political coordination and organization, and (4) of scientific technology. The statistical use of psychological material offers to the student of politics large areas hitherto unexplored, and insight into springs of political action up to this time only imperfectly observed.

From time to time the study of politics has been completely abreast with the current science of the time, as in the days of Aristotle, and from time to time has drifted away again into scholasticism and legalism of the narrowest type. Writers like Wolff and Thomasius, Suarez and Pufendorf, Woolsey and Sidgwick, have left us great monuments of industry and erudition. They, like many others, were of great value in the general rationalizang process of the time, but were sterile in the production of living theories and principles of political action. In our day the cross-fertilization of politics with science, so called, or more strictly with modern methods of inquiry and investigation, might not be unprofitable.

In the study of international law, for example, may we not go behind treaties and conventions into a deeper study—not only of what are commonly called social and political forces, into differences of environment, language and culture—but also into a systematic examination of race and group loyalties and aversions, their genesis, strength, their modes of adaptation and organization? Instinctively the stranger is the enemy. But what has modern political science to say about the nature of this instinct and the possibilities of training, education and reorganization of it? What have the world's students of politics and kindred sciences to say upon this problem, the solution of which bears so closely upon world organization and world peace?

We have studied the urban problem in terms of "good" and "bad" government, of boss rule and reform, of innumerable mechanisms and contrivances ingeniously devised, but is it not possible to go more deeply into the basis of the city, scrutinize more accurately the social and political process of which the political is an integral part? Are the

forces producing municipal misrule inherently re-
calcitrant and insuperably unruly, or do we not
fully understand the political reactions in the given
environment, and how they may best be educated
and constructively adapted to new modes of life
under the forms of the cooperative enterprise of
democracy?

In the study of public administration may we
not add to the study of rules and laws and forms
of procedure and control some deeper insight into
the underlying factors affecting and conditioning
personnel and organization and operation of large
groups of men? Will not the methods of statistics
and psychology be of service to us in the prosecution of such inquiries?

In short, may we not intensify our study of the
political man, the political personality, of his genesis, environment, reactions, modes of adaptation
and training, and the groups of which he is a part,
and of the complicated political process, to a point
where the preconceptions of politics will be given
a far more definite fact basis, and practical prudence a far surer touch in its dealing with the
problems of state?

We may be reminded of the weird anthropology
in the politics of Bodin and Montesquieu, or of
Bluntschli's fearfully and wonderfully made "po-

litical psychology," in which he compared sixteen selected parts of the human body with the same number of organs of the body politic, or of the ambitious but abortive social physics of Comte, or of the array of organismic theories which Dr. Coker has so comprehensively catalogued—all these to point the danger of advancing beyond the line of strictly authoritarian or tendential and prudential politics. But on the other hand we may point to many penetrating studies in social and political organization. We may call attention to the surprising practical advances made by criminology and penology, and to the daily practical applications in social and industrial relations of information and methods drawn from the newer disciplines.

Must we conclude that it is possible to interpret and explain and measurably control the so-called natural forces—outside of man—but not the forces of human nature? Or have we overdone "nature" and underdone "man" scientifically? Is there some fundamental line of division between the cultural, the humanitarian, the scholarly, the "learned," on the one hand, and the scientific (in quotation marks) on the other, so that their methods must be fundamentally different? Perhaps it is so.

It is now nearly thirty years since the great naturalist Le Conte pointed out that art comes first, then science; then science like a daughter helps the mother. Hitherto, said he, "Social art has advanced in a blind staggering way, feeling its way in the dark, retrieving its errors, recovering its fall." But this cannot longer be. He continues: "Science must be introduced into politics only as suggesting, counselling, modifying, not yet as directing and controlling." Science "ought to be strictly subordinate to a wise empiricism. She must whisper suggestions rather than utter commands."[1]

For our purposes it is not necessary or possible to read the future of social or political science. It is sufficient to say that we may definitely and measurably advance the comprehensiveness and accuracy of our observation of political phenomena, and that the processes of social and political control may be found to be much more susceptible to human adaptation and reorganization than they now are.

Here we are confronted, however, as at other points by the urgent practical necessity for better organization of our own professional research. It would be possible, both nationally and internationally, to coordinate much more closely the scattered undertakings in charge often of isolated observers and workers. The political research of our nation and of others is ill-organized, especially for a branch of knowledge that deals with organiza-

[1] In Brooklyn Ethical Association, *Man and the State*, 351–353.

tion and administration as one of its central topics. As a result, even though the available forces are small, there is some duplication of effort. There are large gaps left where there is no investigation made, and there is general lack of organized effort to break through the lines of political ignorance and prejudice. We lack comprehensive and forward looking plans, following which we might advance by measurable stages in certain directions at least. If the mortality among students of politics is high because of the ravages of university administration and politics, there is all the more reason for husbanding carefully our resources, and making the most effective use of them. And if the endowment of political research is more difficult because it must compete with other objects touching less closely, or seeming to, the nerves of the social and political order, there is all the more reason for explicit statement of definite plans and for continued pursuit of the means to carry them out under public or private auspices.

These suggestions are offered in conclusion:

1. More adequate equipment for collection and analysis of political material;

2. More adequate organization of the political prudence of our profession;

3. The broader use of the instruments of social

observation in statistics, and of the analytical technique and results of psychology; and closer regard
to and relations with the disciplines of geography,
ethnology, biology, sociology and social psychology;

4. More adequate organization of our technical
research, and its coordination with other and
closely allied fields of inquiry.

Quite properly a bill of particulars might be
called for, but this paper is only in the nature of
a declaration, and specific statements are the next
step in the case. What has been said is wholly vain
unless it has been understood to emphasize above
everything else the crying need for organization
and coordination of effort both in general method
and with specific reference to the activities of our
professional societies.

Science is a great cooperative enterprise in
which many intelligences must labor together.
There must always be wide scope for the spontaneous and unregimented activity of the individual, but the success of the expedition is conditioned upon some general plan of organization.
Least of all can there be anarchy in social science,
or chaos in the theory of political order.

2 The Foundations of the New Politics

The last century has witnessed profound discontent with government. At first this uneasiness seemed due to the arbitrary nature of the older forms of monarchy and autocracy, but when the *ancien régime* had been destroyed, there was still restlessness and dissatisfaction with organized government.[1] Anarchism boldly attacked all organized authority; guild socialism and syndicalism endeavored to "depoliticize" society and free autonomous groups from its control; in somewhat the same spirit communism assailed democracy. Direct action and dictatorships grew in favor, even among the intelligent. The methods and the mechanisms of parliamentary government aroused universal attack.[2] The courts and the law to a dangerous extent lost their prestige as Solomon-like interpreters of the common ideas of justice. Large groups of persons lost interest in things po-

[1] Summarized by Willey in Merriam and Barnes, *History of Political Theories, Recent Times*, chap. ii.

[2] Best stated in Bryce, *Modern Democracies*.

84

litical, or never acquired it, with the result that the power of the professional politicians grew greater than before.[1]

Allowing for the despondency following a catastrophic war, and for the uncertainty caused by the struggles between industrial groups, it is clear that there are deeper causes at work, and that these are fundamental to the existing situation. We are in fact coming into a new world, with new social conditions and with new modes of thought and inquiry, and we may well inquire what direction and form our politics must take if it is to interpret and express these new tendencies of the new world.

It is consequently important to inquire what is the background of the new development in politics, what are the methods that are likely to prevail in the new order of inquiry, and what are some of the possibilities, immediate and more remote, that may arise from the new approach to the problems of human government. It will of course be understood that this is only a tentative sketch, presented for the purpose of suggesting a line of investigation and of eliciting criticism and

[1] Significant studies are W. K. Wallace, *The Passing of Politics* (1924); E. C. Lindeman, *Social Discovery* (1924); "Umano," *Positiva scienza di governo* (1922); A. B. Wolfe, *Conservatism, Radicalism, and Scientific Method* (1923).

further suggestion out of which more useful plans and proposals may perhaps arise. This is, in short, not so much a work of conviction as a challenge; not a conclusion, but a constructive criticism and a forecast.

The background of the new political world is found in a variety of factors, some of which may be enumerated here.[1] One significant situation is the participation of a larger part of the community in the process of government than in previous periods of the world's history. During the greater part of man's experience, the bulk of the population in any political unit was excluded from a full rôle in government, held as slave, serf, subject, or partial citizen. This situation changes rapidly, and with it the alleged necessity of restraint of the mass of the community through unthinking custom alone, or through force and unreason, or through cunningly devised literary or legal defenses of the *status quo*.

Another significant circumstance is the largely increased leisure of the mass of the community. The common lot of mankind has been that of toil to the point of exhaustion, a day ending in weariness, a life unfavorable to reflection. There was

[1] See my "Recent Tendencies in Political Thought," in *History of Political Theories, Recent Times,* by Merriam, Barnes, and others.

little time to give to the problems of state, and the consideration of governmental questions was inevitably very elementary. In recent years masses of mankind have been enabled to attain an extent of leisure without precedent in history, through the shortening of the labor day.

Again, the spread of education is a fundamental feature in the construction of a new attitude toward government. Most of the time, most men have been unable to read or write. Universal and compulsory education advances rapidly and, although far from generally adopted, is on the way toward world-wide acceptance. In the near future everyone will learn to read and write, and the rudiments of what we call an education will be his. The meaning of this development for the process of political and social control cannot easily be exaggerated, for it involves radical alterations in political systems based upon the assumption that most men were not trained to think. The process by which might is turned into right will be a more difficult one in the future than in the past, and the pretexts that once satisfied the casual dissenter will no longer be adequate to silence him, or to furnish the moral stamina for those who attempt to dominate him. The whole basis of political

88   reasoning is rapidly being altered by general education.

Another factor which cannot be omitted from our calculations is the largely increased facilities in communication and transportation, which within the last two generations have transformed the physical world. They have broken down the ancient isolation of men and have put in motion a series of mechanical devices that seem likely to make possible the practically instantaneous communication of every human being with any other.[1] The old world of persons, isolated and incommunicado, upon which ancient political science was built is fast disappearing, and a new one is in process of construction. Older systems built upon outgrown conditions of time and space are hard pressed by the facts of modern life, and cannot sustain themselves. A new sense of international obligation has arisen. The impact of the new forces that are battering at the walls of the ancient idea of the state and the older view of human relations will destroy or modify them.

The democratic movement, the larger leisure of mankind, the broader education of humanity,

---

[1] See J. B. S. Haldane, *Daedalus* (1924). Compare Bertrand Russell, *Icarus* (1924).

the new forms of intercommunication, the larger
resources available for scientific inquiry—these
are factors which are likely to force a readjustment of the bases of the political order, and which
require the development of the technique of government upon a wholly different plane from that
upon which it has hitherto rested. They show not
only a shift in the character of mass thought, but
also a possible reorganization of the standards and
attainments of political reasoning at its most advanced points.

Furthermore, the changing intellectual structure of the time suggests significant advances in
the form and content of political inquiry. Of religion, philosophy, and science we may ask, What
part do they play in the present tendencies in the
political world? It is clear that the importance
of the rôle of philosophy and religion in shaping men's minds politically has declined during
the last generation. Certainly in the political domain their position is not comparable with that
earlier held in the world of political control. Religion during the Middle Ages dominated the whole
field of political speculation and reduced it to theological politics. Speculative philosophy took possession of politics during the seventeenth and eight-

eenth centuries and held its grip until the eighteenth, when it took its final form in the highly abstract "metapolitics" of the mid-century. Religion seems less effective politically in the modern world than in the centuries that have immediately preceded us, or in the more remote periods of human existence when religion and government were difficult to disentangle, and when the king and priest were one. Writers of the type of St. Thomas and the eloquent Bishop of Meaux, philosophers of the significance of Locke, Hobbes, Hegel no longer are able to impose their classifications and categories upon the human mind in the field of government. This is not to say that imposing figures are not found in commanding positions in our time, but to indicate that their rank is less significant than in previous generations, and that they are apparently less adequate to meet the problems of the modern world.[1]

By far the most significant of the intellectual developments of the time is that which goes under the somewhat unsatisfactory name of "science." In this field we come upon revolutionized types of thinking, whose application has transformed in-

[1] This topic is more fully discussed in the chapter on "Recent History of Political Thinking."

dustrial processes and the modes of human living.[1] In the fields of chemistry, physics, and biology, the advance of scientific method has been very rapid, so swift, indeed, as to leave few of the ancient landmarks standing. These discoveries have furthermore been utilized through mechanical appliances, by which they have wrought fundamental changes in the structure of industrial and social life. Among the more significant consequences have been the large increase in the control of man over the forces of nature, the release of human energies from manual toil, and changes in transportation and communication that have revolutionized the nature of human intercourse.

Science has been no respecter of traditions or conventions, of authority however ancient and well established. The more venerable the established tradition, the louder the acclaim when it fell before some newer discovery. Science did not respect the commands of religion or regard the prohibitions of the law if they crossed its path toward the truth, but moved steadily onward toward its goal.

Human nature, however, was not so thoroughly

[1] Useful studies are those of W. Libby, *History of Science;* F. C. S. Schiller, *Studies in the History and Method of Science;* W. C. Curtis, *Science and Human Affairs;* E. G. Conklin, *The Direction of Human Evolution.*

explored as nature; in fact, a line was drawn between them, as if one were in one world and the other in another. The natural and the "unnatural" sciences were differentiated. This was due partly to indifference, partly to difficulty found in developing truth in the social field, and in some cases to a conviction that it was impossible to arrive at exact truth in the field of social relations.[1] The study of human nature was not, however, without its significant advances in the recent period. It is a hundred years since Auguste Comte published his *Positive Polity*, a systematic attempt to establish a social science. Here are found the beginnings of a definite science of society, corresponding to physics or chemistry—"social physics," as Comte himself termed it. Comte did not, in fact, carry out into practice his own methods, but instead developed a type of politico-religious mysticism and idealism, which finally landed him in a "religion of humanity" and a crude piece of political contrivance. What survived was not his somewhat fantastic and certainly unscientific scheme of a world-state, not the cult of Comte, but the suggestion of and the impulse to the scientific study of social phenomena.

[1] This position is well stated in Max Weber, *Gesammelte Aufsätze zur Wissenschaftslehre* (1922).

In the last half-century, outstanding contributions to the inquiry into human nature were made by history, economics, statistics, and psychology.[1] Likewise biology, anthropology, geography, and engineering made significant advances toward the border line of the social field, and made it necessary and desirable to reckon with them in the formulation of social and political conclusions. The significance of these advances may be very briefly appraised at this point, recognizing that it is impossible to give a full account of them or to make adequate recognition of their respective contributions.

History contributed, in contrast with the abstractions of the seventeenth and eighteenth centuries, the importance and the value of considering the genesis of institutions. With the discovery of evolution in the biological world, the historical concept of change and development coincided, and henceforth the two ideas were found working together in the interpretation of the past of humanity.[2] That history tended to glorify tradition and to strengthen the predominant social and political group, or to supply rationalizations for those who held or sought power, cannot be contested,

[1] See chap. ii for more detailed discussion of this topic.

[2] See Barnes's *The New History and the Social Studies.*

and in many of its aspects it was undeniably closely allied with nationalistic and other forms of propaganda. Notwithstanding this obvious weakness the historical point of view was a valuable one, and tended to raise both the level of general intelligence and the standards of scientific criticism of events.

The most significant development in the economic field was the appearance of the doctrine of the economic interpretation of history and of political and social structures.[1] This analysis of political and social phenomena in terms of systems of economic production was widespread and was powerfully felt throughout this period. It supplied a new point of view and a new method of analysis of human institutions and behavior. Whatever its scientific adequacy, it operated significantly and effectively upon the formation of political and economic judgments, and must be ranked among the formative influences of the century.

Two significant agencies of inquiry were also developed and to some extent applied during this period. These were statistics and psychology. Statistics appeared in systematic form almost simultaneously with Comte's project for a science of

[1] See E. R. A. Seligman, *Economic Interpretation of History;* C. A. Beard, *Economic Basis of Politics.*

society, and during the latter part of the nineteenth and the earlier part of the twentieth century developed with great rapidity.[1] The mechanism of quantitative measurement of social data was improved, and the interpretation of social facts was attempted in many directions. The use of such data forms a striking contrast to the earlier forms of discussion and proof in social and political studies, and this development is unquestionably of far-reaching significance in the evolution of political science.[2]

Psychology during this period advanced from a speculative philosophy to an experimental science, from introspection to objective measurement.[3] Here we encounter the beginnings of a more acute analysis of human traits and behavior and the development of a special technique for measurement and comparison of traits, and of the special conditions under which differentials in these traits are produced. This was true not only of mental testing or measurement, but also of other branches of psychological study, such as the psychiatric phases of the science. It is too early to make any useful estimate of the ultimate value of

[1] John Koren, *History of Statistics.*

[2] See chap. iv, "Politics and Numbers."

[3] See chap. iii, on "Politics and Psychology."

the psychological method, but it seems to contain large possibilities for the more accurate understanding of the fundamental traits of human nature, and to open out broad avenues of approach to some of the situations hitherto most baffling to the world's thinkers. It is too early and it would be too easy to assume or conclude that psychology holds the key to all the problems of politics, but it offers at any rate what now seem like golden possibilities to the student of the social sciences.

Significant progress was also made by the geographers who in the nineteenth century, under the leadership of von Humboldt and later of Ratzel, undertook the systematic study of the physical features of the earth and its climate. In its later forms geography took on the aspect of social geography, and began the study of institutions as influenced by their physical environment. Thus geography occupied a middle position between geology on the one hand and social organization on the other, endeavoring to interpret them to each other. Political geography was also undertaken during this period.

Likewise notable advances were made by the anthropologists and ethnologists who pushed the lines of human knowledge far back of any point reached in previous periods, and who also under-

took the more intensive study of the habits and
characteristics of different ethnic groups. Systems
of measurement began to be applied (biometry or
anthropometry) and to be used for determining
some of the fundamentals of the various racial
groups. Some of these efforts were chiefly refined
propaganda of various groups, but there was also
something of scientific method in the process, and
significant advances were made when all is considered.

During the nineteenth century engineering rose
to a position of great importance in the world of
mechanical construction and enterprise, where it
won notable victories in large-scale accomplishment and in remarkable feats of ingenuity and precision. Later the engineer began to turn his attention not only to the physical material from which
great structures were built, but also to the human
material out of which great enterprises are wrought.[1]

Out of biology also came ideas significant for
the political and social development of mankind.
The remarkable discovery of Darwin began a fruitful period of biological interest and discovery, and
made it possible to advance the bounds of human
knowledge in this field far beyond the most daring

[1] See the Introduction to the report of the Federated American
Engineering Societies on *Waste in Industry* (1921).

imagination of earlier days. Among the subjects of importance developing here were the intensive study of population, the inquiry into the differential characteristics of various groups (differential biology), and the practical development of what came to be called eugenics. The latter signified a possible means of reorganizing the physical basis of the race, and of immense advance in the improvement of the stock of humankind.

It is in the light of these advances in history, sociology, economics, statistics, psychology, biology, engineering, anthropology, and ethnology that the present and future development of political thought and scientific method must be considered. Social changes of the type described and advances in intellectual technique have made a new world. What will be the type of the new politics that meets the needs of the new social and intellectual world?

It is not the purpose of this brief sketch to do more than outline in briefest form the recent developments in the intellectual world that seem likely to influence the future growth of political and probably social science. Yet even here the question may be raised, What have these inquiries to do with the study of law and government? What place have they in the advance of political science?

Is it feasible to consider these new disciplines in relation to politics, or does this place too heavy a burden upon the shoulders of the inquirer in the field of government?

This may be answered in the first place by asking if it is possible for politics to go on without them. If we consider immigration, or education, or democracy, or imperialism, we must reckon with psychology and with ethnology and with biology. We may put the question the other way. Is it possible to study politics or to solve governmental problems in ignorance of the results of these new developments? These forces are already in the field of government. We need not go out to meet them. They have come and are with us. Politics will not escape them by hiding its head in the sand.

Inevitably the new politics will be a new synthesis, in which elements from the older and the newer disciplines will be brought together and articulated and organized. An intelligent study of human government will reach out for all the materials developed and made available by the researches of mankind, and will make them a part of its system, discarding what is no longer useful and absorbing what is desirable and beneficial.

That the mass of mankind now participate in government, that their leisure has been vastly increased, that they are equipped with universal education, that transportation and communication have revolutionized the time-honored conceptions of time and space in politics—these are considerations that mightily influence the politics of the future. That history has developed; that economics has lent its aid to the study of government; that a science of society has begun to develop; that statistics and psychology are available as methods of inquiry; that biology, anthropology, engineering are all at work on the fundamental problems of human organization; that religion and philosophy have relatively declined in their hold upon the political mind, and that science has greatly increased its sphere of influence—these are facts with which political research must reckon. All these are considerations of fundamental importance in judging the tendency of the future development of politics. They indicate that the earlier prevalence of unreasoning habit, of brute force, of transparent rationalizations of those who have or seek power, are on the decline and are likely to be supplanted by widely different kinds of knowledge of the science of government.

The new technique of the new time must be adapted to the new background, social and intellectual, of the new world in which we live. Politics as the art of the traditional advances to politics as the science of constructive, intelligent social control. The new world demands scientific knowledge to deal with the new world-forces that are being unleashed. Propaganda and pseudo-science will not be able to provide adequate government of the world in a period where stability and order and morale are more important than ever before in the history of man. The politics of the new world into which we are coming must correspond with the rest of its life. It cannot be a thing apart, surviving from a pre-scientific period. Politics must reckon with a new world which in time and space are fundamentally altered; a new world of universal leisure; a new world of universal education; a nontraditional state of mind; a world of scientific methods and results; a race of beings master of nature's forces in greater measure than before dreamed possible; the participation of the bulk of the community in its fundamental conclusions.

What form of government these changes, more revolutionary than any that ever shook France or Russia, will bring, I shall not undertake to predict. But some of the possibilities in the development of the science of government will be considered.

Furthermore, we must face the fact that the world possesses two great mechanisms of control that have never before existed in the same form or with the same possibilities of effective use. These are education and eugenics, which are likely to play a greater rôle in the government of mankind than have force and tradition in the past. They are the most powerful figures looming up in the world of social control. One is already established; the other is in the making.

Education, universal and compulsory, is about to envelop the world, and has already encompassed the Western nations It may be conceded that much of modern education is crude and imperfect; but nevertheless, with all its imperfections, the school stands out as one of the great organs of social cohesion and social training. It takes the child for a steadily growing period, for steadily longer hours, for a steadily widening series of subjects, and it tends to reach beyond the school age into the field of adult education and development. Its mechanisms are the subject of the most intensive study and are constantly being revised and strengthened by an army of workers whose lives are devoted to the most minute and thoroughgoing inquiries. The results of a genuine science of government we may reasonably expect will be utilized by this powerful agency of civilization and government.

Eugenics is far less fully developed than education as a mechanism for social and political control, but it is advancing at a rapid rate,[1] and the
time cannot be far distant when its methods will
have wide vogue in every developed community.
It may be possible to predetermine in considerable
measure the types of person desired in the commonwealth of the future, negatively at first by forbidding certain unions and later by constructive
measures in which compulsory processes need play
no rôle. This was foreseen and described by Plato
in his *Republic*, but the subsequent development
of physiological and biological science has not been
such as to permit its practical application, and
even then not in the form conceived by the Greek
thinker. The conscious determination of the character and quality of its people would impose upon
every system of social control a burden which it
has in large measure hitherto avoided. We must
face this situation, however, and its possibilities are
fraught with immense significance for the weal of
the race. This power will mean that the results of
scientific politics may be put into effect with greater certainty and swiftness than has ever been seen
before. If we learn definitely the traits and types

[1] See S. S. Holmes, *The Trend of the Race*; W. E. Kellicott, *The
Social Direction of Human Evolution*.

of men, we may then determine what traits and types we shall encourage and foster, and which we shall direct our energies systematically against.

It is through education and eugenics, then, that future social traits may be determined, perhaps to an extent that would now be considered chimerical or impossible even. The new politics must reckon with them as the older did with unreflective custom, with force, and with rationalizations, religious, philosophical, or legal, designed for the special occasion. Medicine, psychology, and even biochemistry may come to the aid of these agencies in determining the course of their activity, or in holding the track that has been determined upon by the state.

Whether we recognize the situation or not, we are very rapidly approaching a time when it may be necessary and possible to decide not merely what types of law we wish to enact, but what types of person we wish to develop, either by the process of education or of eugenics. If the methods and the processes of social treatment develop as rapidly in the next generation as they have in the past, it may be possible to produce almost any type of individual, subject to the biological limitations imposed upon him at birth. And if the science of eugenics should ever advance as rapidly as it has among animals, to say nothing of plants, it may be possible to determine what sorts of creatures are to be born, within important limits at least. Under these conditions the democracy, or whatever the form of government may be at that time, will be obliged to determine far more fundamental questions than have ever been entrusted to the decision of any governing agency in the history of the race. On what sort of data and by what method of political reasoning, when this time comes, will we approach the settlement of these momentous questions?

It is idle to say that such questions are never likely to arise, for at this very time the problem of race restriction has been determined in America, in crude fashion it is true; and the world is shaken by the propaganda, open and secret, of groups basing their programs upon race and class hostility, often of the most unscientific kind. In the new world made over by modern science, such problems and others equally or more complex will inevitably arise, and will require for their intelligent solution a different political science from any we now possess. Fundamentally, the new politics is likely to be scientific and constructive, forward looking rather than traditional, authoritative, and retrospective. This is not to say that the precious experience of the race will be thrown away, but to indicate that there is a wide difference between history as the artistic embalming of tradition and as the scientific knowledge of the past evolution of the race, considered with reference to the conscious direction of future evolution. Geological history, for example, does not petrify, but on the contrary releases the forces it discovers. Likewise in politics we may study the growth of political control, not for the purpose of ancestor worship, but of more intelligent control of the process of government.

3 Recent History of Political Thinking

The purpose of this survey is to examine the development of methods of inquiry in recent years in the field of political science and of the related social sciences. It is also proposed to examine specifically the advance made in methods of the study of government in the United States. And, further, it is proposed to sum up the principal advances in method in the study of government and the chief remaining obstacles.

An adequate analysis of recent political thought requires at the outset a look at the fundamental factors conditioning the intellectual processes of the time. Here if time permitted we might sketch the outlines of the larger social forces of the time, such as industrialism, nationalism, urbanism, feminism. We might examine the larger group interpretations as seen in the theories of the middle class, of the business group, or of the labor group, and we might scrutinize the rationalizations of the several race groupings of the time. Any thorough inquiry would necessitate some such wide-sweeping view of the forces that so profoundly affect the character and method of political thought. For present purposes it will be assumed, however, that such an inquiry has been made and that its results are fresh in the mind of the inquirer. It would also be desirable and necessary to examine the general intellectual technique of the time as reflected in philosophy, in religion, and in science. Obviously it is necessary for the purposes of such a discussion as this to assume that this survey has already been made. We may then advance to a more minute inquiry into the methods of political thought in the narrower sense of the term. It will be necessary to advance with great rapidity in order to cover the ground within reasonable limits of time, but it is hoped that it may prove possible to sketch the main outlines of the development of recent political thinking adequately for the purposes of considering what methods are now open to the use of political scientists, and what the relative advantages of these methods may be.

METHODS IN RELATED FIELDS

The development of methods of inquiry in related fields of social science is so intimately associated with progress in the study of government that advances in the various social disciplines will be briefly sketched at this point.

Politics has been placed under obligations to economics during the recent period of development.[1] The classical and historical schools of the first part of the nineteenth century were continued and expanded, but new forms of economic speculation came into vogue. The climax of the classical school was found in the writings of the British economist, Alfred Marshall, who while in many ways eclectic in his theory may perhaps most accurately be characterized as a neo-classicist. The historical school found noted expounders, particularly among the German thinkers, in the writings of Wagner, Schmoller, and others. In the main, however, these thinkers continued the development of the classical and historical types of economic reasoning already begun in the first half of the nineteenth century.

In the meantime there appeared the Austrian school of economics, evolving the doctrine of subjective value, or what might loosely be called psychological values. In the writings of Wieser, Menger, and Böhm-Bawerk, emphasis was shifted from the earlier forms of analysis to another aspect of the economic process which they called the subjective and which some others term psychological. Here we have an attempt to interpret economic

[1] See L. H. Haney, *History of Economic Thought.*

values in terms of mental attitudes, suggesting, but by no means realizing, the later developments of psychology.

Following the Austrian school came the study of economic motives, instincts, tendencies, or traits; in short, the inquiry into economic behavior.[1] These inquiries were by no means complete; in fact, they were characteristically inchoate. Their chief significance thus far is the emphasis laid upon another aspect of economic thinking. These scattered inquiries mark, as in the political field, the beginnings of another line of observation and reasoning.

From another point of view the science of economics developed through a statistical, or at times even a mathematical, method. Economic statistics were worked out more rapidly than any other form of social measurement. This was due undoubtedly to the stress of business requirements and opportunities. The application of these measurements was direct and evident, closely concerned with the profit-making and quantity-production system of the day, and the result was the accumulation

---

[1] See W. C. Mitchell's notable discussion of "Quantitative Analysis and Economic Theory," *American Economic Review*, XV, 1; J. M. Clark, "Economists and Modern Psychology," *Journal of Political Economy*, XXVI, 1; Z. C. Dickinson, *Economic Motives;* R. G. Tugwell (ed.), *The Trend of Economics.*

of great masses of statistical analyses, often of the very highest value and significance. To be sure, the surveys of the past were more common and more accurate than the estimates of the future, but the latter began to find a modest place in the calculations of the more daring economists.[1]

The doctrine of the economic interpretation of history, developed in the middle of the nineteenth century by historians and economists, was a subject of further analysis and application.[2] Loria, following Marx, undertook an interpretation of institutions in terms of economic interests and forces which, while not very skilfully executed, was symptomatic of general tendencies. The socialist group in general utilized the doctrine of the economic basis of politics for purposes of class propaganda. Generally speaking, this emphasis upon the economic factor in social life found wider and wider acceptance among the students of politics.

There was a pronounced tendency, however, to inquire into the social and psychological causes of. events as well as the more strictly economic. It became evident that unless "economic" was used as an all-inclusive term covering the whole material environment, it would be inadequate as an expla-

[1] W. M. Persons, *The Problems of Business Forecasting.*

[2] See E. R. A. Seligman, *The Economic Interpretation of History.*

nation of human behavior in all instances. While
it was frequently asserted that men reason in terms
of their economic interests, seldom was the question raised as to what determined their precise
type of thought. Obviously the interpretation of
the same economic interests might differ and even
conflict, in which case the reason for the variation
must be sought elsewhere than in the economic
force itself and might lie in the forms or types of
thinking. If out of exactly similar economic situations diametrically opposed conclusions or widely
varying types of reasons were developed, it is clear
that some other factor than the economic interest
must have entered into the forces that produced
the result.

The study of history during this period developed materials of great significance to political
science, although its influence is not as notable as
in the second and third quarters of the nineteenth
century. At that time the historical method had
swept the field both in jurisprudence and in economics. The German historical jurisprudence and
the German national economics had illustrated in
a striking fashion the influence of the historical
method of inquiry. In this period the historical
influence was unquestionably dominant, although
toward the end of the era it tended to weaken and

decline where it was supplanted by processes of actual observation and of psychological and statistical analysis.

History itself was profoundly influenced by the same set of forces that were gradually changing the character of the study of government.[1] The conflict between romanticism and positivism in this period was vigorously conducted, but on the whole the idealists seemed to yield to the attacks of the historical realists or materialists. Buckle, Ranke, Lamprecht, and in America writers of the type of Turner recognized the influence of mass, races, societies, economic and social tendencies in determining the course of historical events, and they reached out with great avidity for illustrative material of different types. History ceased to be purely military or political, and tended to become either economic or social history, while in some instances historical materialism triumphed completely and the course of events was interpreted altogether in terms of the action and interaction of environmental influences.

[1] See G. P. Gooch, *History and Historians in the Nineteenth Century;* Croce, *Theory and History of Historiography,* especially chap. vii on the "Historiography of Positivism"; Shotwell, *History of History;* F. J. Teggert, *Processes of History* (1918); John C. Merriam, "Earth Sciences as the Background of History," *Scientific Monthly,* January, 1921; Barnes, *The New History and the Social Studies.*

While these tendencies appeared, the bulk of historical writing, however, was still under the older school of the mid-century; in the main, political narrative with some deference to the influence of social forces, but often without any very searching analysis of these factors or any technique other than of critical documentation. The historian could distinguish the genuine writing from the bogus, or he could scour the world with immense enthusiasm and industry to uncover hidden manuscripts or archives hitherto unknown. In his critical analysis, however, he waited on the activities of other social studies. At their methods and results he was not infrequently prone to cavil or complain.

From the point of view of political science, however, an immense amount of institutional political history was uncovered and made available. In the absence of a more definite technique on the part of the students of politics and of an adequate number of observers and students of government, the boundary lines between government and history were blurred, as indeed they must always overlap, so that the technical writing of the history of politics was still in the hands of the historical group. Economists, however, tended to take over the evolution of economic thought and institutions, as did the workers in the field of material science. The review of the scientific processes and forms was completely taken over by the technicians in the various scientific disciplines, as in the case of the history of mathematics, the history of chemistry, and the history of physics.

Significant advances were made in the last generation by the sociologists, who began the study of social organization and process in systematic fashion. While much of the work of Comte and Spencer was abandoned, there remained an impulse toward the development of a science of society, which enlisted the sympathy of many students.[1] The work of Gumplowicz, Ratzenhofer, Simmel, Durkheim, Tarde, LeBon, and, in America, Small, Ross, and Giddings was a notable contribution to the understanding of the social process. For the sociologists a central problem was that of social control, to which political control was incidental and collateral, but inevitably the study of the one subject threw light upon the other. Of special significance was the attention directed by these students to the importance of social forces

[1] See H. E. Barnes, "The Contribution of Sociology to Political Science," *American Political Science Review*, XV, 487; Albion W. Small, "Sociology," in *Encyclopedia Americana*; C. E. Gehlke, "Social Psychology and Political Theory," chap. x in *History of Political Theories, Recent Times*.

and social groups in the development and functioning of political forces, purposes, and institutions. Political scientists of the type of Bodin in the sixteenth and Gierke in the nineteenth century had directed attention to these factors, but they had been somewhat neglected. New interest and study of them was imperatively needed.

The sociologists did not arrive at a very definite social technology, but they struggled hard with the problem and made certain advances of note. The use of the social survey was an achievement of value in the understanding of the social process and tended to introduce more exact methods into the task of social measurement.[1] The frequent use of the case method was also an accomplishment of great utility in the development of the more accurate study of social phenomena.

Of great significance to the methods of political science were the inquiries in the fields of anthropology, ethnology, and archaeology. Here were opened out wide vistas in the early development of the race and in the study of the characteristics of the various groups of mankind.[2] In the field of quantitative measurement, anthropology made

[1] See A. L. Bowley, *Measurement of Social Phenomena.*

[2] See T. L. Myres, "The Influence of Anthropology on the Course of Political Science," *University of California Publications,* Vol. IV, No. 1.

material progress, endeavoring to work out the characteristics of groups by means of physical standards and tests. Even anthropology, however, was often overlaid with race prejudice or with national influence or propaganda of an absurdly transparent type.

A significant development at this point was the rise of anthropogeography. The beginnings of this study may be found in the political science of Bodin in the sixteenth century, as well as in the Montesquieu in the eighteenth. The researches of Ratzel and others in this field were of special magnitude and value;[1] and they were developed and carried on by many students in various sections of the world. In the most advanced form of their inquiries, these students undertook the interpretation of human relations in terms of geographic environment; but this was soon extended to cover more than is usually contained within the limits of geography, and came to include practically all of the factors commonly called social. On the whole, the inquiries were very useful to the study of government in that they tended to shift the emphasis from the purely traditional and authoritarian to the material, the measurable, and the comparable.

[1] *Anthropogeographie;* "Der Staat und sein Boden," in *Politische Geographie.*

In the field of psychology progress was rapid. Advancing from purely philosophical inquiry to standardized and comparable methods of observation, psychology tended to become an instrument of relative precision and uniformity in its application. It was no longer introspective and meditative alone, but developed instruments for making observation standardizable and comparable, and began to make possible a clearer understanding of human behavior, and of what had hitherto been charted as the great unknown in human nature. The significance of psychology for political inquiry was not at first fully appreciated, but in time the results of the psychologists began to be appreciated by the student of government and of social science. Political psychology began to be a subject of discussion, and the terminology of psychology came into common although not accurate use in political inquiry. Psychology began also to find practical application to the problems of government.[1]

In still broader fashion social psychology tried to solve the problem, dealing not merely with individuals, but with the group, or with the intricate interrelations between groups. Here we approach closely the work of some of the sociologists who

[1] See the review of these applications by Harold F. Gosnell, *American Journal of Sociology*, XXVIII, 735. Compare Hollingsworth, *Applied Psychology*.

were interested in the same problem and undertook somewhat the same type of examination.

METHODS OF POLITICAL INQUIRY

Without undertaking a comprehensive review, a brief sketch of the early development of political method may not be amiss at this point. The first methods of political inquiry arc best exemplified in the work of the Greeks.[1] In general their approach to the problems of politics was the philosophical. In the case of Aristotle, however, extensive use was made of the comparison of political institutions, based upon careful collection of available data through political observers. The tutor of Alexander the Great was given by his powerful patron facilities for gathering political facts which have seldom been surpassed. In the Aristotelian process, therefore, it is possible to find material of the highest value. Primarily philosophical in method, he nevertheless used to a considerable extent what we now call the comparative and observational method. It is interesting to observe that in Aristotle and Plato politics looked forward rather than backward, endeavoring to find the form of an ideal state and the means of maintaining it. In Aristotle this was extended to the study of the

[1] See Dunning, *A History of Political Theories;* Gettel, *History of Political Thought.*

methods by which any state might be preserved.

The method of the Romans was primarily juristic in character. They borrowed their philosophy from the Greeks and busied themselves with the tasks of government, administration, and law. In legal science they constructed an edifice which is still one of the intellectual wonders of the world, a marvel of political prudence and sagacity. In the scientific study of government they did not advance beyond the Greeks.

The medieval political theory was legal and theological in nature. The contest between church and state overshadowed the period, and little progress was made in the scientific study of government. The chief stimuli were, in fact, the rediscovered works of Aristotle and the revival of interest in the Roman law. In a contest where logic is the chief weapon, Aquinas, Marsilius, Occam would fare well at any time, but of the verification of hypotheses they remained innocent.

Following the medieval period there appeared signs of important advance in the study of government. This was notably true in the case of Machiavelli and Bodin. The Italian thinker, breaking loose from the theological trammels of the early period, undertook the actual observation of political processes and the development of rules of conduct upon this basis—a process which if continued might have led to significant political progress. Bodin, the greatest publicist of the sixteenth century, sometimes called the Aristotle of the Renaissance, revived some of the methods of the Greek and to these added the study of history as a basis for political conclusions. Likewise Montesquieu in the eighteenth century strove to turn the study of politics into the channels of observation and comparison of actual institutions of government and society, and for the moment while he charmed the European world with his *Esprit des lois*, succeeded in doing so.

All of these tendencies were swept aside, however, with the development in the seventeenth and eighteenth centuries of the natural-law school of political thought, which dominated the minds of men for generations.

The *Naturrecht* thinkers based the study of politics upon an assumed state of nature and the traits of mankind as discovered in this precivil state. But as no such state was found, either in records or by observation, the characteristics of the political man were largely deduced from the imagination or the credulity of the philosopher. This situation furnished a powerful formula for a revolutionary movement. It destroyed the tradition that reflection upon government is treason to the divinely annointed king, and encouraged men to believe that government is a creature of their own will and purpose over which they possess complete control. And to this extent it tended to liberate the human mind from the bonds of custom and tradition. But it did not go far toward the advancement of a genuine political science.[1] Montesquieu, Bodin, Machiavelli were swept aside for the time, and the development of more accurate methods of political inquiry were obliged to await a later day.

The philosophical treatment of politics, firmly established in the seventeenth and eighteenth centuries, continued in recent times, but with less notable examples of logical method than in the eighteenth or earlier nineteenth century. John Stuart Mill's type of political and social reasoning had marked the end of an epoch of speculation among English thinkers, as had that of Hegel among the German philosophers.[2] Bosanquet was an apostle of neo-Hegelianism, while Hobhouse dissected the metaphysical theory of the state. Sorel, an engineer, and Cole, an essayist, discussed political problems in philosophical style, while Bertrand

[1] Some of the psychological implications contained in the thinking of Locke and Rousseau are discussed in chap. iii.

[2] See Mill, *Logic;* Dunning, *op. cit.,* III, chap. iv.

Russell, the brilliant mathematician, evolved a theory of politics. The pragmatists, best represented by Dewey, definitely set about to effect a reconciliation between philosophy and affairs, and to develop a type of logic adequate to the demands of the situation. In the main, however, it is clear that a priori speculation upon political questions was on the decline as compared with the thinking of the eighteenth and nineteenth centuries.

Many thinkers approached the problem of government from the juristic point of view, and primarily their method was the logic of the law.[1] But in many of the leading instances, this attitude was modified by other forms of inquiry. Thus Gierke was essentially a student of the genesis of political ideas. Maitland and Pollock were also deeply interested in the genetic processes of legal development. Von Ihering, with his far-reaching doctrine of social interests, the protection of which is the chief concern of the law, was deeply affected by the social studies of his time, and showed the profound influence of the social science of his day. Berolzheimer was imbued with the influence of social and economic forces in shaping the course of law and government. Duguit was likewise fundamentally

[1] See *Science of Legal Method*, in "Modern Legal Philosophy Series," chap. xi.

affected by the rising study of social forces and of sociology in systematic form. Pound with his sociological jurisprudence is a modern illustration of the same general tendency. Jellinek with the theory of "subjective public law" and Wurzel with his "projection theory" are conspicuous examples of legal logic modified by psychology and by the consideration of social forces.

The study of criminology followed another line of advance, proceeding with Lombroso and his more conservative followers to adopt methods of measurement, to consider the influence of the environment and to statistical analysis, foreign to the speculations of the stricter juristic group, but enormously fruitful in ultimate effect upon the nature of penology. In this respect these studies differed widely from the current type of legal speculation, being founded upon the basis of scientific inquiry rather than upon precedent or the logic of the law.

A frequent way of approach to the study of politics has been the historical inquiry into the development of political institutions.) The modern historical movement began as a reaction against the doctrinaire theories of the French revolutionary period, and swept through the domain of law and government. In recent times it has been a well-traveled road toward political conclusions, and much of the energy in political research has been expended in this field. A survey of the literature of the time shows that the bulk of the output falls under this category. The process of development is employed for the purpose of illustrating broad movements and tendencies of political and social forces, and perhaps deducing certain lessons, morals, or laws from the examination of the past. Thus the previous development of the institution or the people is used to explain its present status or its probable future tendency. In these situations the history of political ideas or customs or forms or institutions becomes the background for the consideration of its present situation.

Another method has been that of comparison of various types of institution, with a view of classifying, analyzing, discovering similarities and dissimilarities in them. Here we have a study of comparative government or law which, while using historical material, is not confined to an inspection of the genetic process, but employs contemporary material as a basis for political reasoning. Industrious researches of this type have been carried on in recent years both by jurists and by students of government. Kohler is a conspicuous example of the juristic group and Bryce of the other. Freeman, Seeley, Sidgwick, Hasbach, Laband, and many others have employed similar methods. In general, description and classification are developed in this way and certain useful comparisons and analogies are set up.

With the comparison of types there came to be a body of political science centering around the observation and description of actual processes of government, as distinguished from historical development or from comparisons of existing types of organization and structure. Much of Bryce's work fell under this head, as did that of Ostrogorski, Redlich, and Lowell. Bryce's *Modern Democracies*, Ostrogorski's *Democracy and the Organization of the Party System*, Lowell's political contributions, and Redlich's *Local Government in England* are examples of this method of studying government. Many monographic studies of the workings of particular institutions were made in various parts of the world, some decidedly descriptive and structural and some more noticeably analytical. Many of these studies were of course combined with historical inquiries and comparative and analogical researches.

Closely associated with the development of comparison of types and observation of processes was the form of investigation which came to be called the survey. This method of investigation appeared almost simultaneously in economics, government, and sociology. The essence of the survey was the actual observation of forces in operation, with an effort to measure these forces and to standardize some system of measurement. The survey owed much to the engineers and the accountants who contributed materially to its development. The engineer was of course the original surveyor, laying out his lines and conducting his measurements with great accuracy and precision. Surveys of human behavior were also taken up by the industrial engineers, especially in the form of the time and motion studies of the Taylor-Emerson type. Here we have an effort at precise measurement of human behavior in the shape of what is commonly called scientific management. At the outset these studies omitted the basic factor of psychology, but later on they reinstated this essential element in their calculations, although not achieving complete success in this undertaking. The accountant also aided through the analysis of financial data leading to the creation of cost accounting, a process which led to an objective appraisal of human behavior or human services rendered for specific purposes. Thus the accountant and the engineer have given a sharper point to the observation of political forces and processes than it had ever had before.

The social survey was developed by the sociologists, approaching the inquiry from another point of view. Much was undoubtedly due to the efforts of city workers of the type of Booth in London and many other scattered students. The classic type of large-scale survey employing modern methods was the Pittsburgh survey, followed by many others, usually upon a smaller scale. The survey, of course, contained elements of advertising, or publicity, or even propaganda, as well as an element of scientific analysis, and sometimes the advertising features overtopped the scientific analysis, but in the main it directed attention specifically toward concrete factors which were observed objectively and as far as possible measured accurately, analyzed, and compared carefully. In the work of the Sage Foundation, the standards of the survey were materially improved under systematic treatment.[1]

The political survey developed most rapidly in the United States and especially in the urban communities. The large-scale losses and wastes in the expenditure in cities challenged attention, and spe-

[1] See publications of Russell Sage Foundation, Department of Surveys and Exhibits.

cialized grafting was met by specialized analysis
and inquiry for the purposes of community protection. These investigations, while carried on by
trained students of political science, were usually
conducted outside of the academic walls. The
leader in this movement was the New York Bureau
of Municipal Research, followed by many other
similar agencies in Chicago, Philadelphia, Detroit,
and elsewhere. The political survey was the
immediate observation of the operations of government combined with the effort to measure these
operations as precisely as possible and to organize
methods of comparison and conduct analysis of
facts observed. This method was distinct from the
juristic method or the historical method or the his-
torical-comparative method in that it substituted
actual observations of government in operation
and made strenuous efforts toward precise measurement. These efforts were not always wholly
successful, but at any rate they were movements
in the direction of precision. Later, similar undertakings were set on foot by state governments and
by the United States government. In England also
national inquiries of the same character have been
carried through on a considerable scale.

Another group of thinkers approached the
study of government from the point of view of psy-

chology, or of social psychology, bordering upon what might be called political psychology. Of these by far the most conspicuous was the English thinker, Graham Wallas, whose *Human Nature in Politics*, and the later and more systematic study, *The Great Society*, started a new line of political investigation and opened up new avenues of research. It is interesting to compare Wallas' chapters on material and method of political reasoning with the famous chapters in Mill's *Logic* on the logic of the moral sciences.

Wallas, originally a student of the classics, later interested in practical political activity, reacted against the consideration of government in terms of form and structure and undertook an interpretation in terms of human nature. This method of inquiry seemed to involve the development of a type of political psychology. In his *Great Society* Wallas considered political forces as organized around the three fundamental factors of intelligence, love, and happiness, on the basis of which he endeavored to rebuild a political theory and a political structure. In *Our Social Heritage* he opened out still other forms of subtle analysis of political processes, hitherto unexplored.

Wallas' work was brilliant, stimulating, and suggestive rather than systematic. While he dis-

cussed the influence and importance of quantitative measurement of political phenomena, he did
not make elaborate use of statistical data in his
work; and while he continually emphasized the
significance of a psychology of politics, he did not
advance far in that direction. But on the whole
his work was a decided variation from that of his
predecessors or contemporaries, and his impetus to
a new method was a notable one. An interesting
comparison might be made between the method of
John Stuart Mill, that of Lord Bryce, and that of
Graham Wallas, all significant figures in the shaping of English political thought. Walter Lippmann
followed much the same method as his early in-
structor, Wallas, notably in his *Preface to Politics*
and in his *Public Opinion*.[1] Lippmann made wider
use of contemporary psychological advances than
did Wallas, however.

There were also eclectic types of thinkers employing several of the methods just described.
There was no writer who did not employ logic and
history and comparison and analogy at various
times. Even the most dogmatic lapsed into statistics at times, and the most statistically inclined
developed philosophical attitudes somewhat incon-
sistent with the general position of the statistician.

[1] Especially chaps. xxiii–xxviii.

Differences in method were often differences in emphasis and in degree rather than in kind. Nevertheless, the differences were appreciable and significant evidences of the general tendency in methods of political theory. Broadly speaking, they indicate the following to be the chief lines of development of the study of political processes:

1. The a priori and deductive method, down to 1850

2. The historical and comparative method, 1850–1900

3. The present tendency toward observation, survey, measurement, 1900——

4. The beginnings of the psychological treatment of politics

SUMMARY OF ADVANCES AND DIFFICULTIES

From another point of view we may summarize the advances in the study of politics in the period since the vogue of the natural-law philosophy, roughly speaking during the last one hundred years, as:

1. The tendency toward comparison of varying types of political ideas, institutions, processes; toward analyzing similarities and dissimilarities.

2. The tendency toward closer scrutiny of economic forces in their relation to political processes,

in some cases extending to the economic interpretation of all political phenomena. In this, the relative ease of quantitative measurement of certain economic facts greatly aided the process, in fact tending to an extension of "economic" beyond the ordinary usage of the term.

3. The tendency toward the consideration of social forces in their relation to political processes. At times this took the form of a social interpretation of all political facts.

4. The tendency toward close examination of the geographical environment, and its influence upon political phenomena and processes.

5. The tendency toward closer consideration of a body of ethnic and biological facts, in their relation to political forces.

6. These influences taken together set up another relationship between political phenomena and the whole environment, both social and physical. Crude analogies of this kind had already been made by Bodin and Montesquieu, but these were by no means as fully developed as the later and far more minute and searching inquiries.

7. The tendency to examine the genetics of political ideas and institutions. This was the joint product of history and biology with their joint emphasis on the significance of historical growth and

development and of the evolutionary theory of life. Since the middle of the nineteenth century, it has operated powerfully upon all political thought.

8. The joint tendency to combine a view of the environment (economic, social, physical) as a whole with the genetic or evolutionary point of view may be said to have effected a profound and indeed almost revolutionary change in political thinking. Certainly this is true in comparison with the static doctrine of scholasticism, or with the absolutistic tendencies of the *Naturrecht* school of thought.

9. The tendency toward more general use of quantitative measurement of political phenomena. On the one side this took the form of statistics or the mathematical analysis of political processes. The great agency through which this was brought about was the census, which prepared great masses of material for the use of the observer and the analyst. Two disciplines in particular were able to apply the quantitative methods with especial success. These were anthropology and psychology, in which domains notable advances were made in the direction of measurement.

10. Political psychology was foreshadowed but not at all adequately developed during this time.

These tendencies taken together may be said to constitute the most significant changes in the

character of political thought down to the present
day. Significant defects in the scientific development of the study of government are as follows:

1. Lack of comprehensive collections of data regarding political phenomena, with adequate classification and analysis.

2. Tendency toward race, class, nationalistic bias in the interpretation of data available.

3. Lack of sufficiently precise standards of measurement and of precise knowledge of the sequence of processes.

Some fundamental difficulties in the scientific study of political processes are readily discerned.

1. The paradox of politics is that group discipline must be maintained in order to preserve the life of the group against internal and external foes; but that rigid discipline itself tends to destroy those vital forces of initiative, criticism, and reconstruction without which the authority of the group must die. There must be general conformity with the general body of rules and regulations laid down by the state, otherwise there is no advance upon anarchy; but there must also be reasonable room for freedom of criticism, for protest, for suggestion and invention within the group. Obviously the position of science in this situation has often been a difficult one, either because of a conscious clash

between group interest and science, or because of an unconscious drift away from the lines of scientific inquiry.

2. The difficulty of isolating political phenomena sufficiently to determine precisely the causal relations between them. ⟩We know that events occur, but we find so many alternate causes that we are not always able to indicate a specific cause. For the same reason we are unable to reach an expert agreement upon the proper or scientific policy to pursue, and by the same logic we are unable to predict the course of events in future situations.

3. The difficulty of separating the personality of the observer from the social situation of which he is a part; of obtaining an objective attitude toward the phenomena he desires to interpret. This has been perhaps the chief stumbling-block in the evaluation of the political process. Classes and races and all other types of groupings put forward as authoritative the so-called principles which are the outgrowths of their special interests, unconsciously perhaps interpreting their own interests in terms of universal application. Thus the greater part of political theorizing on close analysis proves to be more or less thinly veiled propaganda of particular social interests. A theory may contain an element of truth or science in it, but the truth will

be so colored by the interests of those who advance the particular theory that it has little genuine or permanent value. The opinions of the most eminent philosophers of a given race or nation regarding the merits of that race or nation are subject to heavy discount, almost without exception. The same thing may be said of the defenders of economic classes or of other types of groups. In the last hundred years, progress has been made in separating the student of politics from his local situation; but the livid propaganda of the war period and the attitude of nationalistic scientists toward each other indicates that, after all, relatively little progress has been made. Not only were political scientists often made propagandists, but they subordinated the work of all other scientists to their purpose, namely, the advocacy and advancement of nationalistic claims.

4. The difficulty of obtaining the mechanism for accurate measurement of the phenomena of politics. Until relatively recent times, most estimates had been rough and uncritical. It is only since the development of modern statistics that anything like accuracy or precision in political fact material was possible. Even now obstacles apparently insuperable are commonly encountered. The development of adequate machinery for the survey

of political forces is still ahead of us. Yet the development of mechanical devices for observation of facts and for their analysis does not present difficulties that cannot be overcome with sufficient persistence, ingenuity, and imagination.

5. A fourth difficulty lies in the absence of what in natural science is called the controlled experiment. The student of physical science constructs a temporary hypothesis which he proceeds to verify if possible by processes of experiment, performed under his direction and control. These experiments he may reproduce at will until he is satisfied of the truth or error of his hypothesis. Such experiments, however, have seemed to lie beyond the reach of the student of political or social science. On the other hand, the living processes of politics are constantly going on, reproduced countless times at various points and in various stages of the world's political activity. It is possible to draw inferences and to verify these inferences by repeated observation in the case of recurring processes. This requires, however, the setting up of more precise machinery than has yet been invented. It is possible that the mechanism for this process may be found in the development of modern psychology or social psychology, which seems to hold the key to the study of types of conduct or behavior, or in

statistical measurement of processes recurring over
and over again in much the same form, and apparently in sequences that may be ferreted out, given
sufficient acuteness and persistence.

POLITICAL SCIENCE IN THE UNITED STATES

With reference to the development of political
science in the United States, we may say that down
to the middle of the nineteenth century there was
no effort to systematize the study of government.
There was the shrewdest kind of practical political
wisdom or prudence exhibited by men of the type
of Hamilton, Madison, Adams, and Jefferson, and
on the juristic side by such masters as Marshall,
Story, Webster, and Calhoun. But of organized
scientific study there was little trace. To this we
may make exception in John Adams' *Defense of
the Constitutions of Government of the United States*,
and Calhoun's *Disquisition on Government*.[1]

The founder of the systematic study of government was Francis Lieber, a German refugee who
came to America in 1827. His *Manual of Political
Ethics* (1838–39) and his *Civil Liberty and Self Government* (1853) were the first systematic treatises

[1] Early types of political theory are seen in Nathaniel Chipman,
Principles of Government (1793); F. Grimke, *Considerations on the
Nature and Tendency of Free Institutions* (1848); Richard Hildreth,
The Theory of Politics (1854).

on political science that appeared in the United States, and their influence was widespread. Lieber was a pupil of Niebuhr, the famous German historian, and was familiar with the German and Continental developments of this period. After many vicissitudes, he became professor of politics in Columbia University. His characteristic achievement was the introduction of a form of historical and comparative method of inquiry into the field of political study.[1]

The next great impetus to organized political inquiry came with the foundation of the Johns Hopkins and Columbia schools of history and political science. The moving spirit in the Johns Hopkins movement for the scientific study of history was Herbert B. Adams, while the founder of the Columbia school of political science (1880) was John W. Burgess. Both of these men were trained in the German universities and transplanted into American soil the characteristic methods of their time. These groups laid the foundation for the modern system of historical and political research, basing them in large measure upon the development of what in Germany was called *Staatswissenschaft*. Out of this movement has grown a long series of monographic studies in the field of gov-

[1] See *Miscellaneous Writings*.

ernment and politics. The establishment of these research institutions was epoch-making in the evolution of the scientific attitude toward political inquiry in this country. They undertook the examination of comparative types of institution, and also undertook inquiry into the genesis of political forms and types. They brought to the study of government for the first time an impartial and objective attitude, and they began the construction of certain mechanisms of inquiry. It may be said that they did not reckon sufficiently, at the outset at least, with economic and social forces underlying the evolution of political institutions, and that they did not fully appreciate the importance of what has come to be called political and social psychology. These developments were reserved, indeed, for a later period, in which there came to be a fuller understanding of economic and social influences, and of the more subtle psychological processes underlying and conditioning them.

In the meantime, a great forward step had been taken in the direction of scientific attainment through the expansion of the work of the United States census bureau, notably under the direction of the well-known economist, General Walker.[1]

[1] See John Koren, *History of Statistics.*

This work of governmental observation and reporting had been begun with the foundation of the government itself, or shortly thereafter, but for the first half-century it made comparatively little progress. Under Walker, the dignity and importance of this highly significant type of large-scale observation was very greatly increased. Large masses of comparable facts assembled with some degree of precision were now attainable for students of government and of the allied social sciences. The American Statistical Society, first established in 1839, was reorganized and rejuvenated in 1888, and gradually increased in numbers and in information. The statistical development in this country remained in a relatively undeveloped state, however, as is the case down to the present time. One of the major tasks of our political science is the survey of the possibilities of political statistics and the development of schedules for extending the domain of statistical information.

The historical and comparative studies remained the dominant types in the United States for many years, and may be said to be in the ascendency at the present time. In this group belongs the bulk of the output of the scientific world.

At the end of the period came the beginning of the study of forces behind government as well as

the forms and rules of government. The work of
Lowell in this field was notable, but was interrupted by his transfer to another realm of activity. Like Bryce and Dicey, he pointed the way to a different type and spirit of inquiry, involving the study of the forces conditioning governmental activity. Like Bryce, he avowed his lack of faith in political principles of universal validity, but like Bryce he alluded on many occasions to the possibilities of political psychology, a domain, however, into which neither of them entered.

The work of Lippmann, a pupil of Wallas, in the approach to a study of political psychology has already been discussed, but may be again considered in its local, American setting. Advancing from the side of government, he approaches the psychologist, moving forward to the position of the the technical analyst of human traits.

Likewise, Herbert Croly, employing the method of philosophical analysis, and utilizing rich social and economic material as background, contributed to a deeper and sounder understanding of political processes.[1]

Some notable developments are discussed in further detail in this study. They deal with the

[1] See *The Promise of American Life*, (1909); *Progressive Democracy*, (1914); *New Republic, passim*. See also H. J. Ford, *The Natural History of the State* (1915).

modus operandi of fact collection and analysis. One of them was undertaken in connection with the work of the law-makers of the state of Wisconsin, under the leadership of Charles H. McCarthy.[1] Another developed in connection with the activities of municipal government, beginning with the work of the New York Bureau of Municipal Research, but later taken up in many other municipalities, more recently in the establishment of the Institute for Government Research, the National Institute of Public Administration, and the Institute for Public Service. These movements are of very great significance, however, in the technical development of the study of government, in that they mark the beginning of an effort to collect fresh material regarding the actual operation of political forces, and also the beginning of a more specific relationship between the theory and the practice of government.

An acute English observer recently expressed the belief that in such projects as these the United States might be expected to blaze the trail toward the development of scientific social research in its highest form. The development of the survey, the tendency to observe and analyze political forces, the increasing appreciation of the statistical meth-

[1] See *The Wisconsin Idea.*

od, the faint beginnings of political psychology are all significant advances in the development of political technique.

A notable variation in the general style of study was the application of the doctrine of the economic interpretation of history to certain phases of American political development. This was seen notably in Beard's works on the *Economic Interpretation of the Constitution*, *Economic Origins of Jeffersonian Democracy*,[1] and *Economic Basis of Politics*. Seligman's penetrating critique of the economic interpretation of history was a notable contribution to the methodology of the time. The significance of these studies lies in the fact that they indicated a tendency to go below the surface of the forms of government and politics, and to examine more ultimate factors and forces influencing the situation.

Another notable development was the study of the American frontier by Turner, in which the influence of the pioneer environment upon the course of history was portrayed. The spirit of revolt against the current methods of historical writing was most effectively represented by James H. Robinson, who broke through the conventional lines of

---

[1] See also the much less critical study of Gustavus Myers, *The History of the Supreme Court*; also A. M. Simons, *Social Forces in the History of the United States*.

historical inquiry, first .n his volume on *The New History*, later in his *The Mind in the Making*. Robinson challenged the traditional purposes of history, writing with particular reference to the undue attention given to political and governmental institutions. In his later work, he advanced a step farther and challenged the validity of the current methods of historical and social research. These protests seem to mark the beginning of a new type of historiography similar to the earlier one in its emphasis upon documentation, but leading out into broader ranges of what may be termed, for lack of a better phrase, social inquiry. Of deep significance was Shotwell's *History of History* (1922).

The beginning of the study of sociology in the United States also influences the course of the systematic study of government.[1] The sociological studies seemed at first somewhat vague and sentimental, but as time went on became more specific, concrete, and more methodical. In the works of Lester F. Ward, the pioneer of sociology in this country, and later Giddings, Small, Ross, Cooley, and others, the sociological point of view and the sociological method became more and more widely influential. Small emphasized particularly the im-

[1] See Albion W. Small, *Fifty Years of Sociology in the United States.*

portance of what he called the "social point of view," by which he meant the consideration of all the social factors in a given situation, as distinguished from the isolated or exclusive consideration of economic factors or political factors alone. Ross, particularly in his work on social control, seemed to veer over toward the study which came to be called social psychology. Giddings was at first interested in the development of the fundamental factor which he called "consciousness of kind," and later in efforts to introduce a degree of mathematical accuracy and precision into the measurement of social phenomena.

The development of political economy was also of significance in relation to political science.[1] Its chief types of inquiry followed the direction of the classical political economy and the lines of inquiry laid down by the historical school. There were notable evidences, however, of the development of statistical method in economics, even taking the shape of mathematical economics; and there were the beginnings of the study of the psychology underlying economic activities. There was also seen, as in the study of government, the tendency toward actual observation of economic processes, developing into types of surveys of sets of

---

[1] Haney, *op. cit.*

148   economic phenomena. Toward the end of the period came the powerful tendency toward vocational training for industry, and toward the development of business or industrial research. Broadly speaking, economics and politics seemed to follow parallel lines of advance, from the a priori method of the classical political economy and the natural-law school to historical and comparative studies of economics or of politics, to statistical inquiries and actual surveys, and on to the study of the psychological bases of economic or political activity as the case might be.

4 Politics and Psychology

The friendship between politics and psychology is an old one. Politicians have always been rule-of-thumb psychologists, and some psychologists have understood the art of politics. Between the developing science of psychology and the newer politics, the relationship is likely to become even more intimate in the future than in the past.[1]

A look backward shows that in the earlier forms of political thinking there were crude types of psychology that are of great interest and significance in the development of the art of political thinking. The ancient philosophers evidently util-

[1] See the writer's article on "The Significance of Psychology for the Study of Politics," *American Political Science Review*, XVIII, 469; Harold F. Gosnell, "Some Practical Applications of Psychology to Politics," *American Journal of Sociology*, XXVIII, 735; Horace Kallen, "Politics as Psychology," *American Political Science Review*, XVII, 181.

Interesting material is contained in W. H. Rivers, *Psychology and Politics;* Graham Wallas, *Human Nature in Politics*, and *The Great Society*. See also the reports of the Round Table on Psychology and Politics, *American Political Science Review*, August, 1924, and February, 1925.

ized all of the psychology that was current in the construction of their political systems.[1]

At the basis of Plato's political theory there was a form of physiological psychology. He set up a correlation between the head, the heart, and the abdomen, and the virtues of intelligence, courage, and moderation; and to these correspond the three classes, the guardians, the warriors, and the workers. Justice is the harmonious co-operation of these three faculties in the individual, and the harmonious co-operation of the three classes in the society. This may seem more like physiology than psychology, but in any case it shows clearly the effort to set up a system of theory on a basis of physical-mental analogy, using such information as was then available.

Aristotle abandoned the Platonic analysis and undertook the task of concrete observation on a systematic scale. Man is by nature a political animal, and therefore the foundation of politics is the normal reactions of men in social life. Thus slavery is a natural institution; the family is a natural institution. So also the state is a natural institution, requiring no other explanation than the observation of human conduct. The ideal citizen and

---

[1] A full account of the growth of psychology is given in the four volumes of G. S. Brett's *History of Psychology*.

the ideal state are means between extremes, rather than balanced types as discussed by Plato. In Aristotle there is little analysis of traits, but the ground is prepared for the objective study of human behavior on its political side. It would have been possible to take the next step in the scientific order and begin the systematic observation of all the so-called natural activities of mankind, and then to classify and analyze these processes more closely.

Machiavelli was the next thinker to begin a direct observation and discussion of human political traits. In his examination of the methods and the psychological equipment of the tyrant, he develops the qualities of cruelty, infidelity, hypocrisy, and suggests alternative types with their advantages and disadvantages, with the keenest insight into political motives and into political behavior. While not as broad in his treatment of types as Aristotle, he excelled the Greek in his minute analysis of a particular system, and in his portrayal of the minutiae of political conduct of certain types, notably the tyrants of his day.

John Locke as a physician was fully abreast of the physiology of his day, just then beginning to develop, and as a philosopher he was fully acquainted with the current theory of knowledge. His of political philosophy was peculiar, he that it began with a natural man in an assumed state of nature. The characteristics of this man were analyzed and described out of hand and without much regard to practical observation. The state of nature he had never seen, and, as he himself said, history comes before records. Hence no one is in a position to say just what happens in an actual state of nature. The philosophers had not arrived at this stage of human development. Under such circumstances, the account of the political traits of men was inevitably very unsystematic, and indeed sometimes very naïve. In general one divested the civil man of his civil characteristics, and then produced the natural man, carefully filling him, however, with all the qualities necessary to bring him back again safely into civil society.

A more elaborate system was that of Hobbes, who by the same method reduced man to a state of nature and then built him up again. Hobbes, however, developed an interpretation in frank terms of appetites and aversions, not wholly unlike what we sometimes call tropisms. He finds three causes of strife: competition, distrust, and glory. He also equips the natural man with a full set of political motives: to seek peace, self-defense, keeping of contracts, gratitude, complaisance, revenge, cruelty, contumely, equity, and so forth.

It is clear that the character of this process

made it impossible to advance rapidly in the analysis of human conduct on its political side. The several writers on natural law each unfolded the traits of the primitive man as he believed they should be developed, but not upon the basis of observation. The systems developed were manufactured from the thinker's imagination of what men were in the time before government was established—a difficult condition to prove, or for that matter to refute, for there was no material for assertion or for contradiction.

Rousseau in his earlier writings endeavored to describe human conduct in the precivil state, but in his later works undertook to interpret politics, not in terms of primitive origins, but in terms of will. The significance of will was evident throughout the social contract. The "general will" was a useful contrivance for his purposes. Will is indivisible, he said; will is inalienable. The general will is consequently a much more useful conception for the maintenance of popular sovereignty than the earlier doctrines of popular rights or power, which might be subdivided or might be alienated. Likewise, the individual will, the official will, and the general will may be set against each other and balanced. In emphasizing will, however, Rousseau started a new line of political speculation, in terms of a trait bordering on the domains of psychology.

It is plain that no scientific progress could be
made with the methods employed by the *Naturrecht* philosophy, for the whole inquiry into political traits was a priori and essentially uncritical.
Contrasted with a political theory which held that
government and governors rested upon divine
right, or that it was treason to think of the bases of
government at all, the natural-law philosophy was
an immense advance; but its limits were soon
reached, and it was difficult to go farther without
retracing the course of political inquiry and advancing by some other way.

With the utilitarians, another method of inquiry was begun. The attempt to interpret politics
in terms of an assumed state of nature was abandoned, and an effort made to analyze conduct in
terms of pleasures and pains. The hedonistic calculus superseded the speculations on the state of
nature. The greatest good of the greatest number
is to be the basis of legislation, and these "goods"
are to be measured and determined by the calculus
of pleasures and pains. Here we have the beginnings of a new analysis of political and economic
motives which proved very useful for immediate
purposes of reform, and started an interesting line
of observation of human motives and traits.

Following this period, elaborate attempts were
made, both before and especially after the Dar-

winian discoveries, to develop analogies between the state and the organism, or between the methods of natural science and those of politics. These have been well summed up in the thoroughgoing study made by Coker.[1]

In more recent times the need of the development of a type of political psychology has been suggested by many students of politics. Thus Lowell says:

> The last generation has made great strides in the study of psychology. . . . . But the normal forces that govern the ordinary conduct of men in their public relations have scarcely received any scientific treatment at all. In short we are almost wholly lacking in a psychology of parties.[2]

James Bryce in all his political writings displayed a keen interest in the analysis of political forces, and in his last work on *Modern Democracies* declared that psychology is the basis of government. "Politics," said Bryce, "accordingly has its roots in psychology, the study (in their actuality)

[1] F. W. Coker, *Organismic Theories of the State.* Compare also David J. Ritchie, *Darwinism and Politics*, and M. M. Davis, *Psychological Interpretations of Society* (1909).

[2] *Government of England*, I, 449. See also his significant presidential address on "The Physiology of Politics," *American Political Science Review*, IV, 1–15, noting that "the subject lacks the first essential of a modern science—a nomenclature incomprehensible to educated men."

of the mental habits and vocational proclivities of mankind."[1]

Better known, perhaps, are the efforts of Graham Wallas to establish the significance of psychology in the domain of political inquiry, especially in his volumes on *Human Nature and Politics* and *The Great Society*. Seldom systematic in his work, the writings of Wallas have been suggestive and stimulating, and have aroused widespread interest in the fundamental basis of the study of political phenomena. Essentially a classicist in training and an essayist in style, Wallas found it difficult to put into actual practice the doctrines he preached, and never made much use of the experimental or statistical methods. His actual contact with political events seems to have given him a sense of realities in the political world that were not being developed in the texts. Toward an interpretation of these realities he was groping.

The writings of Walter Lippmann, especially his *Public Opinion*, indicate a sharp interest in the more minute analysis of political phenomena, best expressed perhaps in his discussion of the "stereotypes" of political personalities and governmental processes and events. From some of the implica-

[1] I, 15. See also chap. xiii on "Traditions"; also the chapter on "Obedience" in *Studies in History and Jurisprudence*.

tions or applications of differential psychology Lippmann has reacted violently, challenging both the validity of the tests as such and their social and political interpretation, if valid.

In recent years psychology has undergone rapid and marked changes. Psychology has been transformed from a largely speculative to a largely experimental type of study, or at least is in the way of becoming definitely experimental. These developments have been especially marked in physiological psychology, in the study of animal behavior, in abnormal psychology, psychiatry, psychoanalysis, in mental measurement, and in behaviorism. In the American Psychological Association the following divisions are found: general psychology, applied psychology, experimental psychology, mental measurement, comparative psychology, and clinical psychology.

There is, of course, the widest diversity among psychologists and among scientists as to the value and significance of the recent advances in this field, and still wider difference of opinion as to the application of the psychological findings. A very interesting development is the recent growth of what is termed "applied psychology," and its application to various parts of the social field.[1] In industry and

[1] H. L. Hollingsworth, *Applied Psychology*.

in government there are many striking cases of the newer uses of modern psychology.[1] Since that time a notable example of the possibilities in this direction is evident in the studies of the application of psychology to civil service undertaken by the Institute for Government Research and on a smaller scale by the National Institute of Public Administration.[2] It is to be presumed that these practical applications will continue, and with the development of psychology and of government will be found upon an increasing scale.

The practical applications of psychology to politics are numerous. From time immemorial those who have practiced the art of political control have employed a rule-of-thumb form of psychology. The general in dealing with his army,[3] the king and the nobility in their relations to their people, the political leader in his effort to sway the electorate, all have studied a certain kind of psychology which they did not call by that name.[4] Napoleon and Lincoln and Lloyd George all understood how to

[1] See Harold F. Gosnell, *op. cit.*

[2] See E. M. Martin, in *Journal of Criminal Law and Criminology*, XIV, 376.

[3] See Émile Mayer, *La psychologie du commandement.*

[4] W. M. Conway, *The Crowd*; Merriam, *American Party System*, chap. ii.

press the secret springs of action; but theirs was not a transmissible art.

Since the rise of modern psychology, the new methods have slowly been adopted by governments for a variety of purposes. In the army, in public administration, in the courts, the devices of modern psychology have been found useful. Probably the most notable example was the use by the United States government during the recent war of the Army Tests designed to appraise the members of the new force of the country. Over 1,700,000 men were given the Alpha or Beta test, with many interesting results.[1] Notwithstanding the violent controversies that have raged around the interpretation of this study, it remains an impressive example of the practical use of a psychological device for purposes of political control.[2]

On a much more limited scale use has been made of psychological tests in civil-service examinations, either for the selection of various grades of clerks or for the rating of police officers.[3] These

[1] These are best given in the *Memoirs of the National Academy of Sciences*, Vol. XV, *Psychological Examining in the United States Army*.

[2] Compare Mayer, *op. cit.*, for the efforts of the French command during the war.

[3] See also publications of the Bureau of Public Personnel Administration, *passim*.

experiments have been only tentative, but they have a value as an illustration of the tendency to apply the psychological method to the problems of government. That the use of psychological measurements in this field is likely to develop seems very probable.

Much wider use of modern psychology or of psychiatry has been made by the courts in the conduct of cases. A very considerable number of courts are now equipped with psychopathic laboratories in which various forms of examination are given for the purpose of aiding the court in making decisions. The value of these helps in dealing with the problem of the juvenile is now scarcely contested, although there is still opposition in the case of adults. Likewise in the determination of responsibility for crime, the alienist and the psychiatrist have been made factors of great significance, although their position is by no means clearly defined at present.

Suggestions have been made as to the importance of more scientific analysis of evidence presented in court, but thus far almost no steps have been taken in this direction. What the future holds here is purely speculative, although not without interest to those who look ahead into the future of our juristic machinery. Whether modern methods may not revolutionize the standard procedure of ascertaining the truth by the process of oral argument is of course a question which cannot now be answered. The legal rules of evidence have been built up through long years of trial and error and neither will nor should be given up unless it is clearly shown that a superior method is available. For this the psychologist is not prepared, and perhaps may never be.

In the army, in the court, in the administration, in the various forms of custodial institution, in the school, the modern methods of psychology have penetrated, with varying success. The indications are that other and more notable advances will be made with the development of psychology in other lines. Enough has been indicated to show that the practical relations between politics and psychology are not only those of the older rule of thumb, but also tend to follow the lines of scientific advance.

One of the phases of psychology that has attracted the widest attention is that of mental measurement, and that because of the numerous generalizations that have been drawn from some of the tests that have been made. Education, citizenship, immigration, democracy all are vitally affected by some of the conclusions that have been drawn from the work of mental testing, whether rightly or wrongly. It must be said, however, that most of the dogmatic assertions regarding the bearing of differential psychology on democracy have been made by those who were neither students of government nor of psychology, and consequently not qualified to deal with either subject, to say nothing of the far more difficult problem of applying one to the other.

The validity of the mental measurement process has been seriously called in question by many in the field of professional psychology. Whether the measurements test ability any more accurately than records of performance or achievement; just what quality it is that they really test; the limitation of the validity of the tests either because of their verbalism or their adaptation to special sets of circumstances, as the schools—all these are technical challenges made by technicians, and I shall not undertake to discuss them here.[1] Questions affecting the application of these tests to government and to education have been sharply raised in the acrimonious controversy between Terman and Lippmann, and also between Whipple and

[1] An interesting analysis of the meaning of these tests is given by F. N. Freeman, "A Referendum of Psychologists," *Century Magazine*, December, 1923.

Bagley.[1] It is, of course, impossible and unnecessary to follow these controversies through all of their logical and psychological windings here. It is perhaps sufficient to point out for the purpose of this inquiry:

1. The tests thus far made do not show whether the "intelligence" rated is the product of environment and training, or whether it is a characteristic unalterably fixed at birth, and either not subject to modification or to very slight modification.

2. These tests do not show, thus far, the relation between the differentials in intelligence and the kind of capacity that is essential for the purposes of political co-operation and organization in governmental association.

It must, of course, be recognized that there is still an unsolved problem arising, in part, from the fact that geneticists and environmentalists are carrying on types of work of a highly technical kind, but very inadequately co-ordinated, and therefore relatively unfruitful in certain directions. Nor are we yet informed as to the transmission of acquired characteristics. Until some of the fundamental situations in this controversial field are set-

[1] G. M. Whipple, "The Intelligence Testing Program and the Objectors Conscientious and Otherwise," *School and Society*, XVII, 561.

tled, it will be difficult to draw dogmatic conclusions regarding the complex political and social characteristics of mankind.

Both of these limitations are important considerations in applying psychological conclusions to the problems of political science. Obviously, if general intelligence is a product in great measure of social environment and training, or if the general intelligence measured has no very intimate relation to political intelligence and capacity, the tests have a relatively different significance.

It is, broadly speaking, difficult to discover thus far any conflict between differential psychology and democracy, in any sound interpretation of the theory of either; but that will be considered in another place, and time does not permit extended discussion on this occasion. The rôle of inheritance in predetermining social and political traits, as far as our knowledge goes, seems less significant than the part played by social training and environment. In all probability many of the political characteristics of various groups do not go back far in biological inheritance, but are the products of a generation of sophistication in the habits of a particular group. That political ability or capacity is packed in the original chromosomes, as some hasten to conclude, and transmitted from generation to generation, we have yet to prove, if it can be proven at all. Most of what has been written thus far about race political characteristics is twaddle or transparent propaganda, which should deceive no one not under the spell of some form of political hysteria. But if it be shown that political ability follows any such fixed laws, it may then be possible to ascertain what these laws are, determine the conditions under which ability or the lack of it arises, and shape the course of the race accordingly. Eugenics is racing along as fast as mental measurement, and may keep pace with it.

If we reach a point where by scientific process we can breed and train what types of man we would, it does not seem that we should breed and train 3 per cent of geniuses and 97 per cent of morons. We should probably contrive a more balanced society, with some in advance and some a little behind, with plenty of room for variation in the freak and sport, but leaving the mass of human beings on something like a democratic basis. There are myriad lines of development open to men and women, and the leaders and followers in one cycle need not be those in all cycles of advancement and preferment. Hence, men may be simultaneously superior and inferior in many ways and relations, commanding or leading here and following or obeying there.

Of course, if there are hereditary variations so deeply rooted that they can never be changed, so specifically political as to be significant, we must accept them as a new form of political fatalism. The biologist or the psychologist will have brought about what Plato said must be taught in his system once and for all, the divine lie as to the origin of inequality and the basis of status. In the meantime we need not take too seriously the lies that are not divine.

Mental testing is not the only part of the psychological field that touches upon politics. Psychoanalysis and psychiatry have an important bearing upon certain phases of political life and conduct. Physicians have learned much from the study of the abnormal type, and possibly students of politics might profit likewise by similar types of study. In criminology it is true that important use has been made of this principle, and it is significant that great progress has been made by reason of the insights thus obtained. Every court and every custodial institution recognizes this fact in the most evident manner. In the other fields of government we have not made equal use of this possibility. We have, to be sure, some studies of the boss and the grafter, and occasionally a pseudoanalysis of the radical or the rebel or the conservative; but these inquiries leave much to be desired in the way of thoroughgoing and scientific analysis. Sharp analysis of subnormal and supernormal types of citizen and official might yield useful results in the understanding, not only of the abnormal, but also of the normal type of citizen. A shallow and speculative form of political psychiatry would, of course, be of little value, except for the sensation-monger, but careful collaboration with the psychiatrists might enable us to understand better some of the significant phases of our civil life; and we might include the physician, as well, in the combination. In judicial and criminological work, in the treatment of defectives and dependents, there can be no doubt that the use of the psychiatrist will be very greatly extended and increased in social and political significance.

From a scientific and from a practical point of view it is important to keep our eyes open to the large possibilities in the co-ordination of medicine, psychiatry, psychology, and political science. Out of such a series of converging interests and disciplines there may come types of social diagnosis and prognosis that may have far-reaching consequences in human behavior, and which may vastly increase the possibility of intelligent social control. In modern communities these factors are somewhat loosely organized at present, but they contain potentialities that cannot be overlooked; and likewise in the scientific field, there are highly interesting vistas of progress in this direction.

Another significant field is that of animal behavior and of child behavior. The study of the subhuman types and the facts of their organization and association have been partly developed, and hold fascinating possibilities for the student of government. Forms of order and precedence were established in animal groups long before the state appeared, and in these early types may be seen significant forecasting of the *homo politicus* as he later appears in the course of evolution.[1]

Likewise in the study of the child are found opportunities for the observation of the political attitudes and interests of the later citizen. Here on a simple scale are written large many of the characteristics that later become effective in social and political life. Judging from a few inquiries that it has been possible to make, and others forecasted, the examination of the rise and development of the political ideation and the political behavior of the child has in store for us much of value in the scientific understanding of the adult idea and conduct. In the juvenile group, furthermore, we may readily observe the forces that create, modify, and destroy

[1] W. M. Wheeler, *Social Life Among Insects.*

the earlier types of belief or behavior. This is an
unexplored field of which it is necessary to speak
with reserve, but it appears to contain material of
the very greatest value for the searching study of
political and social control. And we cannot say
that we do not have facilities for observation.

Another important aspect of the case is the relation between psychology and social psychology.
Thus far, studies have been made chiefly of the response of the individual to external stimuli. But
it will not be long before the question will arise as
to the nature of these stimuli, the nature of the
groups or the associations out of which the individual comes and which in large measure shape him.
In short, we deal not merely with individuals in
studying the whole process, but with groups of individuals or societies of individuals; and we must
deal with the relations between individuals and
groups, and between groups. We must deal with
sets of relations which are as real and as capable of
study as the reactions of the individual alone. We
are studying tropisms of various types, or responses
of various types, and these are social as well as individual. At this point experimental psychology
will come into contact with social psychology,
which has started at the other end of the line and
approaches individualistic psychology. Unfortu-

nately, social psychology has, thus far, made relatively little progress in the direction of experimental work. It has often been content to dwell in the field of speculation in relation to the nature of the social organism or social soul or spirit, much of which is metaphysical, or, as Dunlap puts it, metabiological in character, and relatively unfruitful of development. In other cases the social psychologist has advanced only as far as certain large categories, such as imitation, suggestion, consciousness of kind, conflict, compromise, and many others of similar type. In other instances, instincts have served the same purpose.[1] While these analyses have often been suggestive and stimulating, they have not led much beyond this stage, and it may well be that they are not likely to do so.

Up to the present time, it must be conceded that the development of social psychology has left much to be desired. It is, in the main, still in transition from the old-time philosophy to the newer and more concrete experimental type of science. It is evident that the relation between political problems and those of social psychology is very intimate, and that the maturity of social psychology contains great promise for the students of what may be termed political psychology. The relations

[1] See L. L. Bernard's careful study, *Instinct*.

between men in the political process are not individual primarily, but social. They are reactions, responses, tropisms that are the result of social situations and of social training and experience. To study them as if men existed in a vacuum is to study man as ineffectively as those who wrote elaborate but sterile treatises upon the state of nature and the natural man in the seventeenth and eighteenth centuries. It is especially deplorable that the use of precise measurement in social psychology has been so largely neglected, and that the controlled group has been so little utilized for purposes of experiment.

It may be asked, Is it not possible that the real relationship of students of politics is with biology or neurology rather than with psychology? Do we yet know what changes may be wrought in the individual through biological modification or through biochemistry? How far may attitudes and behavior be influenced or determined by biochemical processes which we do not yet thoroughly understand, as for example through modification of glands, physiological functions, or neural mechanisms? To what extent is it possible to condition and determine these attitudes by conscious biological or biochemical processes? Is it possible that we may make a leader or a rebel, or a good citizen, or a warlike attitude, or a pacific attitude, by biological or biochemical process?

May political methods in time be materially modified by any of these processes which confessedly are still vague and ill understood? These processes are now so little understood as to be of little practical value for the study of politics. But they are being studied with great intensity, and it is by no means improbable that very remarkable progress may be made here in the not distant future.[1] If, as, and when they appear, it will be necessary to deal with them, and it is not impossible that they may play a significant rôle in the politics of some future time. It is by no means out of the question that they may develop more fundamental conditions than are disclosed by any of the processes of psychology. Already we recognize the influence of physiological conditions upon individuals, and govern ourselves accordingly in fixing legal responsibility and punishment. The scrutiny of biological conditions underlies modern theories of criminology, and it may well be extended, as knowledge of these processes expands, to other situations in political society. They may underlie leadership and servility, radi-

[1] A. E. Davies, "The Influence of Biology on the Development of Modern Psychology in America," *Psychological Review*, XXX (1923), 164-75.

cal and conservative, aristocrat and democrat, good and bad citizen, and a wide variety of political attitudes and types of behavior. We can by no means ignore their basic relation to the fundamentals of political conduct. Crudely suggested in the early studies of Plato, they have largely been neglected in the subsequent studies of political life and behavior.

In a practical way we have long been familiar with the effect of such devices as the war dance, the pipe of peace, the political rally. We know that the "bad" boy may be suffering from bad teeth, or may be hungry; we are aware that very simple operations or changes may work large changes in the conduct of individuals or perhaps, on a larger scale, of groups. But the scientific possibilities in this domain are largely unexplored.

The question may be raised, At what points is there most likely to be contact between psychology and political science? No one can, with any degree of confidence, forecast the development of either science during the next generation, but nevertheless certain probabilities exist, and to some of these attention may profitably be directed. These probabilities or possibilities lie along the borderland between psychology and politics.

It seems probable that mental measurement

will be still further developed, to include not only what is now called intelligence, but other qualities, as disposition or temperament. It is possible that we may find room here for political qualities and characteristics of certain kinds. Moore's study of aggressiveness, Pressey's studies of temperament, Downey's tests of will and determination are interesting examples of this. Further studies of judgment, insight, balance, leadership, conformity, and so on may be developed with time and patience, and if worked out will throw much light on the characteristics of the political man. The political scientist and the psychologist may readily co-operate at this point, one suggesting the qualities it is desired to analyze, and the other supplying the mechanism for measurement. Of course a political scientist trained in measurement could himself carry through the testing process, which after all is a relatively new one without the long history of some other techniques. There is hope that in this field of analysis of traits and qualities interesting and important discoveries may be made in the course of a little time. Closely connected with this work is the study of attitudes of the individual. Significant illustrations of this are the recent studies of Hornell Hart in the field of international attitudes. Many other forms of analysis of this general type may readily be instituted and are likely to be forthcoming in the near future.

Another significant field where early contact is likely is the study of political interests. These may be examined with reference to their direction and strength, and also with regard to their genetics. At what time and under what situations do political interests arise, how are they manifested, and under what situations do they acquire strength and direction? Some pertinent inquiries have been made on a small scale in this direction, and with good results. On a larger scale such investigations might help us materially in our understanding of the political man and of the motivation of political conduct. What are the factors that create political interest or activity, or tend to destroy or modify it? To what extent may these factors be controlled or modified? What is the relation of political interests to other social interests and to other factors in the individual's composition?

Here two suggestions may be made with a view to strengthening the inquiry. One is that patterns of traits, habits, responses, behavior may be traced, and in this way political personalities may be charted out in some detail. It is by no means always true that a single trait characterizes the man or the group, but rather a series of traits in combination,

or a series of combinations of traits. The knowledge of this plan or pattern aids in understanding
the general direction and speed of the type. It is
possible to select the type of the man or group in
such fashion as to surpass any present system of
appraisal of political types. What we now know
about the conservative, or the radical, or the liberal, or the rebel, or the aristocrat, or the democrat,
or any one of many other types may be much more
definite if time is taken to make the tedious but
indispensable survey preliminary to the conclusion.
Both Plato and Aristotle undertook the analysis in
crude form thousands of years ago, but their task
has never been continued in the light of modern
facilities for observation and analysis.

In the next place, it is possible to set up many
forms of correlations between individual traits,
group traits, or individual or group patterns, on
the one hand, and other factors that are measurable and comparable. Sex, race, economic status,
education, mobility, physical and mental qualities
are only a few of the facts that may be related to
the qualities in question, or the types of behavior
under consideration. Under what circumstances,
in other words, do the differentials in political
character or conduct develop? In what ways may
character and conduct be modified and adapted by

shifting the circumstances? Repeated observations and analyses of this type ought to reveal more than we now know of the situations under which political characteristics are shaped and reshaped.

In fact, the way is open to large-scale statistical studies and correlations of political conduct, with a rich variety of types of physical, psychical, and social fact, both on the side of heredity and of environment, and in the light of the relations between them. There seems to be no limit to the points of approach to this inquiry, and there seems to be an indefinite possibility of obtaining scientific knowledge of how the political man is really constituted and modified.

As social psychology develops, the whole study will be correspondingly enriched by the addition of the analysis of groups, of group relations' and individual-group relations, and indeed the whole interlocking series of cycles in the complex social process. Discussion of whether the group is or is not an organism, or is or is not an entity or a reality, or has or has not a soul or a spirit will not advance us much farther or faster now than in the Middle Ages. But intensive studies of community organization, in which units of measurement and comparison are employed, will promote the understanding of the social process with which the political process is so intimately bound up.

In recent conferences on the relationship of politics and psychology, many suggestions have been made regarding specific lines of inquiry offering promise of scientific achievement.[1] It is urged that collections be made of political biographies and autobiographies. Personal observation, introspective analysis, narratives and accounts of all types are the indispensable material out of which political science may be built. Unfortunately, however, we have only the scantiest store of material of this type in specific case form, available for scientific study. The mere collection and analysis of such material is not perhaps essentially scientific, but it will bear fruit in suggestions of the very highest value for further inquiry. Out of such material should come suggestions and insights, hypotheses, of the very greatest value in opening out new lines of inquiry, in developing new methods of attack on the problem of the human political personality and conduct. This work may represent the pre-Darwinian stage in the evolution of science, but it is apparently a necessary and in-

[1] See *American Political Science Review*, February, 1924, 1925, and *passim*.

evitable one. Suggestions developed as a result of such collections of material might be taken up by psychologists or by students of politics, or by both, but either is likely to be aided by the presence of an abundant store of such data.

The specific types of inquiry suggested included a wide range of topics in which it seems probable that fruitful experiments might be made, and in fact a number of them are under way at the present time. Among the more significant of the fields indicated were those concerning change of opinion as influenced by persuasive material of various kinds, and the effect of various factors such as nationality, race, sex in affecting willingness to change or rate or direction of change. Studies of public opinion and of various forms of propaganda were also suggested as likely to develop valuable results. Analyses of leadership might also be followed through by psychologists and students of politics working together.[1] Studies of the traits of citizenship[2] and analysis of political vices and virtues lend themselves to certain types of scientific study. Obviously the significance of these conferences did not lie in the discovery of finalities in methods of approach, but in the beginnings of the

[1] See the writer's Introduction to Gosnell's *Boss Platt*.
[2] See D. S. Snedden, *Civic Education*.

necessary process of attention to more strictly scientific method.

These are, of course, only types of inquiry, and merely indicate a long list of possibilities. The psychology of the parliamentary and electoral processes, many psychological aspects of administration, the analysis of many juristic situations— these present interesting fields of inquiry and may well be made the subjects of examination in the near future.

From a scientific point of view the advantage of such inquiries is twofold. They make possible the construction of comparable units of measured action, and they set up specific and minute studies of political behavior. These are, therefore, if properly conducted, double advances toward intensity of inquiry and toward results that are comparable. They contain elements of great value in the development of political measurement and comparison, out of which the knowledge of relations may be derived and from which a science of politics may be built.

It is clearly evident that it is desirable and indispensable to develop a much more intensive study of human nature on its political side, and that psychology offers one way of analysis that seems to hold rich possibilities. This need not and will not be the only type of analysis, but it seems likely to give to politics many interesting and important lines of advance. Human nature, the *terra incognita* of the political and social philosophers, may be more fully explored than has hitherto been possible. Whether psychology becomes a general science of human behavior or, like statistics, a method of approach and inquiry in the hands of students of government, industry, and education, is relatively unimportant in view of the goal which is in view—the understanding of political and social relations.

In this work the practical co-operation of students of politics and of psychology may be of the very highest value. The student of politics is not, as a rule, master of the psychological technique just now in the process of development, and on the other hand the psychologist has not perfected his mechanism, nor is he usually very fully informed upon the problems of the political scientist. The psychologist cannot at one and the same time lay down the canons of industry, of government, of education, mores, and morals. He will seek the co-operation of students in the several disciplines upon which his science borders, or where his inquiries lead. The farthest-seeing psychologists are fully aware that they cannot go where they would like without the fullest study and development of the social and political implications of the human nature they have undertaken to study. Furthermore, psychological technique is still largely in the making, and special forms and applications are likely to spring up in several parts of the field, as in industry, education, and government.

It may be said that the lines of inquiry suggested are not appropriate for political scientists, because they carry us out of our accustomed territory, and we may be lost in the desert. The same thing may be said with equal pertinence of the psychologist dealing with such material. In any case a certain number of explorers must always be lost, especially if they advance too far or too fast. It is not, after all, of primary importance whether we call the work psychological or political, or both, but it is of fundamental importance that it be done by someone, however named. Politics cannot live and flourish upon the abstractions surviving from the natural-law philosophy, or the historical roots of institutions (which are not without nourishment), or the stimulations of legal logic. If politics is not to be the residuum left after all ascertainable facts have been exhausted, or the literary rationalizations of those who have or seek power, so well exemplified in the funeral orations of Bossuet, it must adapt itself progressively to the new intellectual technique of the time. During the last century politics learned to take cognizance of great historical, economic, and social forces, in the seventeenth and eighteenth centuries much neglected. This was a memorable achievement. It is equally necessary now to examine the new insights into human nature offered by modern science working in psychology and biology and other fields. The new politics will be a synthesis of many elements now found in the older and in the newly developing disciplines. Of fundamental significance is the new point of view and the new method afforded by what we call psychology; and politics can no more ignore it than we can ignore history or economics in their respective fields. What we are really striving to achieve is neither psychology nor psychiatry as such, nor biology as such, nor history as such, nor economics as such, nor statistics as such, but the development of scientific method in the observation, measurement, and comparison of political relations.

Wherever we find comrades in this quest for truth—and is not the search for realities in the social field the greatest need of our day ?—why not welcome them and catch step without examining too closely or too long their pedigrees or their passports?

5 Politics and Numbers

There are doubtless many to whom the topic "Politics and Numbers" suggests the tax rate or the election returns, numerical analyses familiar to many groups in every community. To others, "political" statistics may recall the juggling and adroit manipulation of half-understood facts. Others may see in politics and statistics the exact antipodes— a world of inexact opinion and a world of precise measurement, separated by a great and impassable gulf.

However this may be, politics and numbers have been intimately associated for many centuries of their common existence. Numbers at the outset were magic symbols, with a mystical potency of their own, a spell that might greatly influence governmental relations.[1] Plato declared that the number of citizens in the ideal state should be 5040, because this number was exactly divisible by 59 divisors, and therefore possessed magical qualities.

[1] "Here is wisdom. Let him that hath understanding count the number of the beast; for it is the number of a man; and his number is six hundred three score and six" (Rev. 13:18).

He demonstrated that the tyrant was 729 times less happy than the just ruler, because this figure is the cube of 9. As tyranny is the perversion of the three qualities of intelligence, courage, and moderation, this gives the cube, of course. This is a case of Egyptian mathematics operating on the mind of the learned Greek. The otherwise wise and judicious Bodin, in the sixteenth century, likewise resorted to the mysticism of numbers to support his political conclusions.[1]

The early writers upon politics, however, made little use of numbers in drawing their political principles. Their chief method was that of logic or of observation of common occurrences, and the massing of figures in support of a contention was foreign to their style of argument. None of the later writers of the major significance of Locke, Montesquieu, Rousseau employs in consideration of political problems any array of figures. Their works are almost barren of reference to quantitative measurement of political events. The lawyers used the logic of the law, the logicians the refinements of dialectics, the historians the citations of chronology, but only a few references were made to measurements of the political data they were discussing with such power and eloquence. Philosophy, the Fathers, history, the Roman law, the Scriptures

[1] Book IV, chap. ii.

186   are all familiarly encountered, but not the detailed tables of figures with which we are now familiar. Had there been a disposition to employ them, the collections of data that we now call statistics would have been largely wanting.

The method most commonly employed in politics has been that of observation, development of shrewd hypothesis, and attempts at verification by observation, but without any special effort in the direction of numerical or statistical analysis. This is the way by which Aristotle, Machiavelli, Bodin, Montesquieu, Bagehot, Bryce, and others endeavored to arrive at political conclusions. Very often they reached results that are attributable to the insight of a skilled observer. They might almost be called political psychiatrists.

Thus Aristotle says: "There are two parts of good government: one is the actual obedience of citizens to the laws; the other part is the goodness of laws which they obey."

"As virtue is necessary in a republic, and in a monarchy, honor," Montesquieu finds, "so fear is necessary in a despotic government."

Rousseau observed: "The strongest man is never strong enough to be always master, unless he transforms his power into right, and obedience into duty."

Hobbes declares that "reputation of power, is

power; because it draws with it adherence of those that need protection."

Machiavelli observes: "And let it be noted that there is no more delicate matter to take in hand, nor more dangerous to conduct, nor more doubtful in its success, than to set up as a leader in the introduction of changes. For he who initiates will have for his enemies all those who are well off under the existing order of things and only lukewarm supporters in those who might be better off under the new."

Out of political practice there has developed a long series of political maxims, sayings, proverbs that are often of very great value in the art of politics. For example, the significance of "moderation," so strongly stressed by Aristotle and later by Bagehot, who used the term "illogical moderation." The importance of the adaptation of the form of government to the characteristics of the people who are to use it is another observation emphasized by Aristotle, Montesquieu, Bodin, Bryce, and others. Other instances are the dangers of excessive division of power and responsibility on the one hand and the dangers of excessive centralization of authority on the other—a theme of numerous political observers, made the basis of many systems of political rhythm or balance of powers.

The combination of good will and ruthless power which is so often found in government, whether of the tyrant, the boss, or the popular leader of the type of Lenin or Mussolini, has frequently been commented upon by the students and observers of political events. How to avoid enemies, and how to make the most of them when they arise, has often been considered by students of government.

These are only a few of the many types of political wisdom that are found throughout political science and practical statesmanship, without much regard to time or place—universal maxims of value everywhere, with variations and amplifications to suit the necessities of special situations in various groups and situations, yet with many maxims common to all.

There is indeed a very considerable body of political lore, made up of the accumulated observations of generations of statesmen and political philosophers, which could be brought together in a manual of the art of government, if anyone desired to do so. Some of the earlier manuals assembled for the use of heirs apparent are good examples, as *Le Télémaque*, compiled by Bishop Fénelon in 1699 for the young Bourbon who was to ascend the throne. A modern manual would differ somewhat,

but would not be impossible to construct from the
sayings of the elder statesmen and the savants.[1]

Shrewd insights of this nature are found everywhere in human life. In medicine, in business, in
prospecting for oil or water or minerals, the
"hunches" or insights of specially gifted persons,
or those with wider range of observation, are of
great significance everywhere. But with the rise
of scientific methods these are supplemented by
more systematic observation and more precise
measurement and more intelligent analysis, on the
basis of which new "insights" again develop. In
medicine, a definite technique develops which re-
places the older methods of the medicine men. The
search for water or oil is carried on by the skilled
geologist. The guess or hunch is everywhere supplanted by the measurement and the analysis. Not
that the insight vanishes, but that a certain field
is taken over by the scientist, and the man with
the hunch or the art moves on.

In the political field the same process is slowly
developing, although resisted here more stubbornly

[1] See the interesting study of Champernowne, *The Boss;* Aristotle's chapters on how to maintain the different kinds of government; Machiavelli's famous discussion of the methods by which the
tyrant might maintain his authority. The Germans term this general
problem the *Makrobiotik* of the state, the art of preserving and per-
petuating power.

than elsewhere perhaps. One of the earlier advances toward political precision is seen in the law, where definition and logical analogy play so large a part. Accuracy is obtained or approximated by sharp definition of the terms employed and by close analogical reasoning from them.[1] This is by no means quantitative measurement, since it turns largely upon the verbalisms employed and upon the analogies set up. It is indicative, however, of a stage of advance in human thinking about social relations. A procedure, a mechanism, and a logic is set up in place of force, irregularity, and inconsistency, however much the procedure may be overlaid with transparent rationalization of power groups. Many aspects of law in relation to social control are indeed not unlike the early relations of medicine to religion.

Some have supposed that the difficulties of politics might largely be obviated by sharper definition of terms, so that the shifting and confusing use of such words as "liberty" and "justice" might be avoided. Lewis'[2] remarks on the use and abuse of some political terms are an interesting example of an effort to put an end to doubt and difficulty in the domain of the political. Unfortunately for

[1] Wurzel, in *The Science of Legal Method.*

[2] *Use and Abuse of Some Political Terms* (1832).

Lewis' plan, his definitions and discriminations were not accepted, and the formation of new phrases went merrily on. While the desirability of more precise use of terms is universally admitted, it is clear that no such general agreement as Lewis sought is possible, nor would it continue if it were reached. Terms often come to have a symbolic value, which may produce direct and perceptible effects upon masses of people, but the scientific question is what is the fundamental basis of this effect, rather than the form of the verbalism itself.

The rise of statistical measurement is relatively recent in the history of the world, and is in fact the creation of the nineteenth century. Originally statistics were concerned primarily with governmental affairs; literally, statistics had to do with the state.[1] The beginnings of modern statistical method are commonly traced to the eminent Belgian student, Adolphe Quetelet, who laid the foundations of modern quantitative measurement in the social field.[2] Since his time rapid progress has been made in the

[1] See Achenwall, *Abriss der neuesten Staatswissenschaft* (1749), deriving the term from *statista*, a statesman. Compare William Petty, *Political Arithmetic* (1690).

[2] See Hankin's monograph, *Adolphe Quetelet*; Bowley, *The Measurement of Social Phenomena*; John Koren, *The History of Statistics*; also Westergaard, "Scope and Method of Statistics," *Quarterly Publications of the American Statistical Association*, XV, 225–91.

development of the technique of the measurement of social phenomena. In the economic field, the pecuniary and profit-making system with its large-scale methods and quantity production was favorable to the minute measurement in terms of money of various economic processes; and very rapid advance has been made in the perfection of the measuring machinery. Accountancy and later cost accountancy led to the close analysis of fiscal operations, and to significant advances in the extent and precision of measurement. The index number,[1] the business cycle, and even the business forecast, with its obvious imperfections, are examples of the strong tendency toward quantitative measurement in the use of economic data.

In the social field important uses of the new method were also devised and applied, notably in the studies made by Le Play of the urban community[2] and later by Booth of the submerged tenth

[1] See Fisher, *The Making of Index Numbers*, chap. xii. See also Moore, "The Mathematical Complement to Economics," *Quarterly Journal of Economics*, XXIII, 1; Persons and others, *Business Forecasting. The Trend of Economics*, ed. R. G. Tugwell, contains significant articles by W. C. Mitchell on "The Prospects of Economics," and F. C. Mills "On Measurement in Economics." Cf. Bibliography, pp. 483–533. See also Jacques Rueff, *Des sciences physiques aux sciences morales*.

[2] A. Reuss, *Frederic le Play in seiner Bedeutung für die Entwicklung der sozialwissenschaftlichen Methode* (1913).

in London;[1] later still in the Pittsburgh survey and other large-scale inquiries in the United States.[2]

Some of the sociologists began the task of systematic use of quantitative measurement and undertook various types of analysis based upon this method,[3] and advanced the lines in this direction for some distance. Guesswork regarding the condition of the poor and the needy was largely replaced by definite information based upon fairly accurate observation and measurement. And, very slowly it is true, there began to emerge from emotion and prejudice a scientific profile or portrait of the community in many of its aspects.

In various related fields the use of types of measurement has been developed within the last century. Anthropology developed anthropometry and there was also produced biometry. Here we find specific measurements of physical characteristics, as the head, its size, shape, angles; the stature, the weight, pigmentation, and various other measurable physical relations.[4] These measure-

---

[1] *The Life and Labor of the People in London.*

[2] *The Pittsburgh Survey* (1909).

[3] See F. H. Giddings, *The Scientific Study of Society*. Compare Park and Burgess, *Introduction to the Science of Sociology*, for a different approach.

[4] See especially, in this connection, the current journals of anthropology, and the large and growing literature of the subject of physical anthropology.

ments are of course confined to physical factors that are perceptible. But in more recent times with the development of psychological testing there has come an effort to determine precise differentials in the field of mental characteristics. In the field of educational psychology especially notable experiments have been made, and in certain cases with significant results. Both in psychology and in biology large use has been made of the statistical method, and in many instances with very important contributions resulting from the process. Some psychologists have been unkind enough to say, in fact, that the statistics of their colleagues were better than their psychology.

Especially significant studies of a statistical nature were made by the biologists, notably by Galton,[1] Pearson,[2] and Bateson.[3] Of especial note were the striking analyses developed by Karl Pearson, which not only attracted scientific interest, but aroused general attention as well. The brilliant work of the biometricians tended to increase confidence in the possibility of the measurement of

[1] *Natural Inheritance: Inquiries into the Human Faculty and Its Development.*

[2] *National Life from the Standpoint of Science* and "The Fundamental Problems of Practical Statistics," *Biometrika*, XIII, 3.

[3] *Biological Fact and the Structure of Society.* See Raymond Pearl, a pupil of Pearson, in *Introduction to Medical Biometry and Vital Statistics* (1923); *Predicted Growth of Population of New York and Its Environs* (1923).

many factors not commonly supposed to be susceptible of such treatment.

In the governmental field, the use of statistics developed with the growth of public finance. In fact, politics was the first of the social disciplines to employ statistics. With the needs of military organization, with the demands of taxation, with the appreciation of the uses of population estimates, with the rise of electoral devices, with the measurement of governmental operations through cost accounting, the governmental statistical service expanded rapidly.

The census is the classical example of the interest of the state in quantitative measurement of political, economic, and other social processes. It marks a long step toward the appearance of science in government, a step the significance of which is but faintly appreciated even now, but which in the long run marks the beginning of a movement of fundamental importance. No one would think of the establishment and development of a bureau of the census as revolutionary in character, and yet from the point of view of intelligence in political control the foundation of such an institution and such a process is of revolutionary significance. It is in the census and in the various statistical divisions of the government that the community deliberately undertakes to find out the measurable facts regarding its social organization, and to initiate the comparison of units of these social processes out of which government is made. At this point opinion, prejudice, appeal to the tomtom and the tradition are for the moment laid aside and search is made for the uncolored facts.

Without raising the more fundamental problems regarding the possibilities and limitations of the quantitative method in dealing with social phenomena, it is clear that there are yet great areas of government in which the established type of statistical measurement has not been applied. And just here is found one of the great opportunities of modern political science, especially in the United States. The development of political reporting is a fertile field for the student of politics. The reports of cities, counties, and states are lacking in uniformity, accuracy, and comprehensiveness, in some instances to the point of the ridiculous. Financial reports are not as a rule comprehensible to the parties in interest, the accountant, the citizen, or the scientist. Reports of many branches of government are unintelligible, and in general they fail to give either the general picture desired by the citizen for the purpose of supervision and control or by the scientist for comparison and deduction.

More evidence of progress is found in vital statistics than elsewhere, but even here grotesque incompleteness in many jurisdictions is encountered. The analysis and constructive criticism of these branches of political reporting is one of the major tasks of students of government everywhere, for it affects the basic facts of political operation, containing the material without which a superstructure cannot be erected intelligently.

The statistical observation by the government supplies to the individual material that he cannot supply for himself, namely, that of large-scale observation with thousands of eyes instead of two. It does for him after a fashion what the telescope does for the astronomer, or the microscope for the naturalist. These observations, moreover, are capable of much greater elaboration than has yet been attained, depending upon the formulation of new types of inquiries capable of being answered statistically.

Notwithstanding the fact that statistics were first developed by the governmental agencies, students of government have been slow to take up the statistical method of political inquiry, preferring the processes of history, description, and the standardized use of the legal methodology. In certain instances they have aided in the formulation of the schedules upon which the statistical information of the government rested, and in this way furthered the development of the measuring machinery available for scientific and other use.

Increasing use of statistical material is made, and constant attempts to interpret and apply such material to the problems of government. Quantitative measurement of all kinds begins to appear in the support of various contentions, hitherto upheld by logic, by analogy, or by history, or by appeal to common observation unmeasured. Illustrations of this will be found in much but not all of the political literature of the last fifty years, as in Lowell, Wallas, and others. The philosophical, historical, and legal groups, however, made relatively little use of the measured fact or force as an element in reaching political conclusions. In writers like Green, Gierke, Tolstoi, Sidgwick, Jellinek, Sorel there is little use made of the material supplied by the modern statistician, or demand for additional observation. On the contrary, the appeal is through analogy, common sense, history, or the literary charm and emotional appeal of the writer. It is only in the twentieth century that the larger use of facts is evident in striking fashion. Then the process of intimate observation, already begun in the nineteenth and preceding centuries, took the shape of the more intensive examination of political processes sometimes called the survey. This was first undertaken in the United States in connection with the government of cities, where was begun the direct observation of the governing process, and the attempt to measure and compare certain units of governmental operation.[1] This work was largely the task of certain agencies known as Bureaus of Municipal Research, active in the institution of investigation and the development of constructive suggestions based upon these inquiries. Similar work was undertaken in England and in other states to some extent, as in Germany, by the governmental officials themselves. Municipal government was an especially fertile field because of the urgency of many of the situations presented, and further because of the absence of powerful traditions of history, philosophy, and law, such as elsewhere make impartial inquiry difficult.

Out of these factors two situations have been established. First, we now possess much greater information than ever before regarding the political and social processes. Incomplete as that information may be, it is far in advance of what mankind has historically had at its disposal. Secondly, the

[1] See R. T. Crane in "Progress Report of Committee on Political Research," *American Political Science Review*, May, 1923.

value of statistical analysis in the treatment of social and political problems has been definitely recognized. No great undertakings are begun in these later days without at least the semblance of a quantitative investigation of fundamental facts. Unsatisfactory as these may be in many instances, yet they mark a significant advance in the method of dealing with social problems, as compared with the appeal to magic, the divinities, traditions, or abstract logic which was careless of the facts. Compare, for example, an argument made by St. Thomas with that of a modern thinker on social questions:

1. The definition of Law.
   Article 1. Whether law is a thing of the reason.
   We proceed thus to the first article 1. It seems that the law is not a thing of the reason. For the Apostle says, "I see another law in my members." But nothing pertaining to the reason exists in the members of the body; for reason does not employ corporeal members. Therefore law is not a thing of the reason.
2. Furthermore, in reason we find only power, mode and performance, etc.
   Moreover, law impels those who are subject to it to right conduct. But to impel to action pertains, properly speaking to the will, not to the reason; thus the jurist says "Quod placuit principi, legis habet vigorem."[1]

[1] F. W. Coker, *Readings in Political Philosophy*, p. 123.

Or the debates of a modern parliamentary body may be compared with those of the same body one hundred years ago, as for example the House of Commons in England or the House of Representatives in the United States. In any case the increasing use of statistical material is clearly evident. I cannot vouch for the intelligence of all of such use, but whether or not, the appeal to the statistical is equally significant of the power of the quantitative measurement over the human mind. Statistics overshadow the Roman law and the Fathers in frequency of citation.

Of fundamental significance is the possibility of future measurement of political phenomena. To what extent may political processes be so far isolated as to make them the subject of precise measurement? Or with what advantage may such quantitative surveys be made? Or what are the limits of such measurements? Evidently measurement has the advantage of setting up a definite unit which, if and when calculated, may be made the basis of comparison with other units or with the same unit under varying conditions. It tends to eliminate opinion based upon general observation or belief, resting perhaps upon self-interest or custom; and to substitute facts upon which there can be relatively little argument. The distribution of wealth and income is not a matter of dispute except as the classification may be contested, if the records are accurately kept. The classification of crimes by race, sex, or economic status may be definitely established, and we may then inquire into the reasons for the differentials. The extent and character of migration may be determined. The housing situation may be definitely explored and measured. In all of these cases opinion is replaced by exact information which cannot easily be contested, except by attacking the method or its practical execution.

When we approach, however, a question such as whether the League of Nations is a useful instrument or not, or whether communism is superior to democracy, or whether proportional representation is more desirable than territorial, or whether prohibition is desirable, we find difficulty in applying the statistical method. Opinion and analogy come into the discussion and largely determine its trend.[1]

This is partly due to the lack of measurement of the practical operations of the proposed systems, and partly to a disagreement as to the values in question or the ends to be served. Here measure-

[1] O. F. Bouck, "The Limits of Social Science," *American Journal of Sociology*, XXVIII, 300, 443.

ment waits upon classification and agreement upon categories, which may be measurable, given time and resources. But the development of these canons of classification is not a rapid process.[1]

Bryce, for example, undertakes to compare democracies by setting up certain standards by which he will measure them all and appraise them. These canons are: security from external attack, maintenance of order, justice, efficient administration, aid to citizens in their occupations.[2]

Here an agreement has been reached, assuming that there is agreement, but upon categories so broad that they are incapable of precise measurement, without much more refinement than is here given. Consequently it is difficult to set up any exact comparison between America and Switzerland or between France and Australia as to "order" or "justice" or "security." It might be possible, of course, to rate states in the order of their assumed value, and then to inspect their various qualities, with a view to determining the correlation between the ratings and the qualities pre-

[1] An excellent example of agreement upon certain classes of facts is seen in the report of the Civic Federation upon *Public and Private Ownership of Public Utilities* (1907), with resultant agreement upon the fundamentals of a report.

[2] *Modern Democracies*, II, chap. lxxiii.

sumed to cause the rank. Probably in this fashion a more penetrating analysis might be made and possibly more definite relations established. A specific example of this type is seen in the attempt, thus far not carried out, to rate cities in the United States and to analyze the qualities peculiar to them by the process just indicated.[1]

In the examination of political phenomena it is possible to discover similarities, some of which are vague and elusive, caught occasionally by a flash of insight, but more likely to be literary generalizations of some rather evident group interest. In certain instances we are able, however, to set up similarities in the form of correlations between sets of data, and thus to approach nearer the truth than is otherwise possible. For example, we may show the correlation between sex and voting, or between economic status and opinion or behavior of certain types.[2] To a much greater extent than heretofore it would be possible by diligent experiment to set up other important correlations, some

[1] See "Reports of the National Conference on the Science of Politics," for such a project in cities, *American Political Science Review*, February, 1924; compare C. H. Judd, *Measuring the Work of the Public Schools* (1916).

[2] For a discussion of the mathematical and statistical use of correlations, see L. L. Thurstone, *The Fundamentals of Statistics*.

of them carrying greater weight with them than others, but, taken together, of material significance in the interpretation of political events and phenomena.

A parallel case is the development of the method of prognosticating weather changes. Pressure areas are observed over a wide range of territory, and from a careful observation of the direction and strength of movements it is possible to forecast, not always with great accuracy, the probable tendencies of the weather. Here is an instance of estimate and approximation, which gives, however, substantial and significant results. In economics this tendency takes the shape of efforts to predict the course of business cycles, now upon a commercial basis, precarious though it may be. The development of modern insurance upon an actuarial basis is another interesting example of the application of the statistical method to a modern problem of life. Even in my day I have known persons who considered insurance as gambling with death or God, as they happened to see the case. Shrewd political observers can usually forecast the outcome of a national election and often of others. For example, in 1924, in 1920, in 1912, 1908, 1904, 1900, there was little disagreement among the "talent" in the United States as to the result. To some extent this forecast was based upon political canvasses and upon the size and enthusiasm of meetings, but also upon the general "drift," or the political "feeling" of the observers. We can predict with reasonable accuracy the number of deaths, the number of crimes, the number of voters, and so on through a list of measurements which are fairly constant.[1]

An interesting example of quantitative measurement is Lowell's study of the extent of party voting. Defining a party vote as one in which nine-tenths of either party voted on one side of a question in a parliamentary body, and ascertaining the number of roll calls yielding such a vote, he determined the percentage of party votes in the passage of laws.[2] With this may be compared, however, the dubious attempt of Woods to set up a correlation between monarchs and their times—studies in what he termed "historiometry."[3] The study of non-

[1] See the interesting study by Edwin Grant Dexter on *Conduct and the Weather* (1899), an inquiry into the effect of meteorological conditions on conduct in New York and Denver. Compare the analysis of the "pressure group" by A. G. Dewey, "On Methods in the Study of Political Science," *Political Science Quarterly*, XXVIII, 631. Interesting types of measurement are found in *Economica*, *passim*.

[2] *Annual Report of the American Historical Association*, I (1901), 319.

[3] F. A. Woods, *The Influence of Monarchs* (1913); also *Mental and Moral Heredity in Royalty* (1903).

voting recently made is another example of the application of the statistical method to the analysis of a governmental situation.[1] The advantages and likewise the limitations of such a study are clearly evident in this instance. A series of such studies carried on under controlled conditions would reveal much regarding the political interests of the voter in different situations.[2] The limitations of such inquiries are evident, but they also contain fascinating possibilities of more precise development and of application in other fields.

It is obvious that there are many obstacles in the development of the method of measurement in dealing with the problems of government. The student of government is confronted with difficulty in determining specific units, and with many variable factors which may make the accurate interpretation of a result very difficult and perhaps impossible. Political situations are usually complex, containing many factors which it is difficult to isolate successfully. The relations of the variables are not always readily disentangled, and

[1] See Merriam and Gosnell, *Non-Voting* (1924).

[2] Ogburn and Peterson, "Political Thought of Social Classes," *Political Science Quarterly*, XXXI, 300; "Methods of Direct Legislation in Oregon," *Publications of the American Statistical Association*, XIV, 136; A. N. Holcombe, *Political Parties of Today*; Stuart A. Rice, *Farmers and Workers in American Politics*; St. Philip's Settlement, *The Equipment of the Workers*.

their confusion may become the source of the most serious error.[1]

The difficulty, however, does not lie, as Bodin once said, in the inscrutability of the human will or in "human nature," although the complexity of mental phenomena increases the difficulty of analysis as compared with the inorganic or the organic but non-social. Nor is it found in the inherent nature of the political process. The real obstacle is found chiefly in the lack of minute inquiry patiently carried out on a small scale, the absence of microscopic studies of the political process carried on in objective manner.[2] While it is sometimes asserted that history does not repeat itself, the political process appears to be much the same in different periods, making allowance for certain variables that must be calculated. Government is a series of tropisms that are likely to recur in the same order or series as much as in any other part of the domain of nature. But those processes must be studied objectively, and not in the spirit of worship of tradition or authority or other disturbing influ-

[1] Compare Giddings, "Societal Variables," in *Journal of Social Forces*, I (May, 1923), 345–50; W. F. Willcox, "A Statistician's Idea of Progress," *International Journal of Ethics*, XXIII, 275–98.

[2] Wheeler in his *Social Life among the Insects* states that 10,000 species of bees and 10,000 species of wasps have been described and studied.

ence growing out of group propaganda or personal interest. When this difficulty is overcome, the mystery may yield as readily as in any other case to analysis based on comparison of measurable units.[1]

We must of course make sure that we are really measuring something, some trait, characteristic, movement, and not merely juggling with figures as such. It is relatively easy to point to institutions, individuals, customs, forms of behavior that are recognized as specifically and perhaps exclusively political in character, as armies, parliaments, courts, administrators, leaders, command, obedi-

---

[1] At this point, I take the liberty of quoting from Thurston (*American Political Science Review*, February, 1925), summarizing the stages of development in the solution of a scientific problem:

"1. A felt social need which requires analysis, satisfaction or cure.

"2. The phrasing of the need or perhaps a small part of it in the form, 'What is the effect of A upon B?'

"3. The definition of the variables A and B, preferably in quantitative form.

"4. The adoption of a unit of measurement for each variable.

"5. The experimental arrangement by which paired observations may be obtained for A and B.

"6. The statistical analysis of these observations to determine objectively the degree of the relation between A and B.

"7. The interpretation which consists in reading causality into the observed concomitance of the two variables.

"8. The formulation of more problems which arise from doubts in the interpretation and from which the cycle repeats itself."

ence, taxes, prisons. But what are the common relations running through these various forms and types? And are they susceptible of measurement? or of isolation? What shall be the units of measurement? What special kinds of tropisms are those which we call political? Do they express any specific or special and exclusive characteristics or cumulation of characteristics that may be scientifically outlined? Thus far, it must be said, they have been chiefly described in terms of themselves, without much progress in exclusion of the irrelevant or non-characteristic. It is of course as useless to say that politics deals with government as it would be to say that government deals with the political. The types of institution or behavior that we call political must be more vigorously defined. Of course the same question arises in all social measurements. In psychology, for example, we may ask just what it is that is specifically psychological, what is the specific factor that may not readily be resolved into simpler elements. To this, thus far, no satisfactory answer has been given by the students of the subject, although the challenge has been made. With the measurement of "intelligence" and other factors of "temperament," the whole problem becomes of course a very acute one.

The same question must inevitably arise when

we begin the task of measuring the political man or the political group or the political process in definite figures. The larger mass movements may of course be quantitatively measured, but what shall we say of the more subtle and elusive traits or characteristics? Will it be possible to isolate and measure them also?

Just when phenomena become political as distinguished from social in the larger sense, or economic or ethical, it is not always easy to say, but the differences are not difficult to detect where they are fully developed. In a sense, any person or institution may become political, and change its aspect at times. The church or the association of commerce or the federation of labor or the racial group may control the state or may transform itself into the state or take on the characteristics of the state for the time, and perhaps for a long time. But observing the social process for a considerable period, the distinction becomes in fact clear enough for working purposes and, what is more to the point, for the purposes of measurement and comparison of the essential processes concerned. In any event, the fundamental problem is that of human behavior, however we may separate its various phases.

The peculiar phenomena connected with war,

or slavery or revolution, or elections, or parliaments or juries or public administration may be studied by themselves for the moment, without losing sight of their fundamental relation to the rest of the social process of which they are an integral part. They are at least as separate as botany and geology, or biology and chemistry, which have integral relations, and in a certain sense are inseparable, but which are none the less distinguishable for purposes of scientific study. And for practical purposes we are not at a loss to find these phenomena or types of behavior available for purposes of scientific study and analysis.

Among these phenomena are the vote, the legislative roll call, the judicial action, the administrative process. Among institutions, we may regard the army, the school, the public personnel. Here are situations teeming with definite facts, susceptible of relationship to other sets of social facts. In the case of public institutions, experiment may be carried out and situations varied for the purpose of determining the effect of the various factors in behavior. No richer material is found than in the domain of political operations. Furthermore, when the minute study of political operations and traits is begun, the number of feasible statistical relationships is of course very largely increased. We can count soldiers, or votes, or tax receipts, or arrests, as well as wasps and bees.

It is not to be assumed that the quantitative study of government will supersede analysis of other types, either now or perhaps at any time. Insight, judgment, analysis are always of value and significance when employed by persons of special gifts or long experience and training or both. They will always continue to lead or to supplement statistical evidence. Indeed, it is these very qualities that are likely to determine the direction of statistical analysis and interpret its significant findings. Just as the psychologist and the psychiatrist are each likely to come upon conclusions of scientific value, so in the political field the statistician using quantitative measurement may discover facts and sequences in one direction and the acute analyst in another, each supplementing the work of the other. But inevitably the observer will tend more and more to use the simpler and ultimately the more complex forms of statistical analysis and will incline more and more toward the precision of measurement that underlies many of our modern scientific discoveries. At the same time the statistical material, from which illustrations may be drawn, will increase from time to time and become available for illustration and argument and, more than all, for discovery of new relations—the goal of scientific effort.

There are those who fear that through statistical measurement political science may disappear in microscopic monographs, isolated, never synthesized, barren in interpretation. Possibly so. It may well be that politics must lose its way before it finds itself again in the modern world of science. This is not unlikely, but after all, this stage is not inevitable.

It is wholly improbable that politics will be absorbed in statistics, and in view of the wide prevalence of mere opinion and assertion in the political world, a strong development of quantitative measurement is desirable. There is little likelihood that the process will be overdone for some time to come. We are more likely to err on the side of the unverified claims of prejudice, opinion, or interest than on that of overemphasis on statistical measurement. There remains even in mathematics a theory or philosophy of mathematics.

The question may be raised whether in the midst of quantitative measurement political theory will not be obscured in a maze of mathematical terminology and method, which may in reality not be strictly applicable. May we not fall short of mathematical accuracy, on the one hand, while losing touch with philosophical speculation on the other? Doubtless some investigators will be submerged in a flood of facts and figures, and perhaps all may be for a time, but there is no necessary reason for the abandonment of theory. The method of quantitative measurement will doubtless be employed in great part for the purpose of verifying hypotheses, of checking up and determining precisely some insight or hunch the thinker may have come upon. Professor Michelson once said that many of his best ideas came to him when he was in a meditative or perhaps even dreamy mood. The ideas were, however, the hypotheses which precise methods were employed to verify or to disprove. What political scientists have too often done was to meditate and then elaborate in literary form an idea, without verification or with very inadequate verification. And possibly the idea was the outgrowth of class or race or personal interest or experience and never had any objective consideration.

It may be really disastrous if political investigators rush into the collection and quantitative measurement of facts without preliminary consideration and statement of what we call the "problem" and without certain hypotheses, not conclusions, which the proposed examination of facts might be expected to prove or disprove, or at least to supply a basis of comparison to other inquirers. There is urgent need in the scientific process of studying politics for meditation, reflection, experience, and for the flashes of insight that come to the fertile mind. What quantitative measurement does is to provide means of checking the validity of the theories, of determining the strength, direction, and relations involved in the assumption. In the course of the inquiry it is quite probable that other "hunches" or insights entirely unanticipated may develop, and these again may become the subject of further inquiry. It is precisely the character of a fertile science that these conclusions and hypotheses continue to evolve in a series that leads to continually advancing precision in the subject under investigation.

The cycle of inquiry, then, is likely to include some preliminary exploration of the problem, some tentative hypotheses, some effort to establish them by analogy (or to contrive others by logic); then the effort to verify by quantitative measurement, and if possible by controlled experiment. Again out of this very process may come new hypotheses which may again be tested and proven or disproven. Or unexpected relations may be discovered while looking for others, as has happened again and again in the field of science. Thus the investigator who started to find one combination discovered another. We say "by accident," but in reality he stumbled upon another relation while in the line of scientific experiment. In like manner the explorer may look scientifically for one thing, and the boldness and thoroughness of his method may unearth something quite unexpected. So the political observer, reasoner, or experimenter who uses a scientific technique will be likely to find situations and relations quite unanticipated, and perhaps—who knows ?—even unwelcome. It is this that has opened a fairyland of adventure to those who seemed only patient fools, half-tolerated under the cloak of magic, religion, and of science or "education."

If the question is raised as to what are the most promising lines of advance in the quantitative measurement of political phenomena, the answer is that there are many inviting possibilities open to the student having time, energy, and resourcefulness. One of the most obvious needs is the development of governmental reporting or statistics. These data are of joint interest to the scientist, the citizen, and the responsible political official. But governmental reports almost everywhere are grotesquely incomplete and inadequate. In the United States such fundamental data as election, criminal, and judicial statistics are available only in the most unsatisfactory form, and there are great gaps in standard statistics that have never been filled. In all jurisdictions there are voids that could be filled, but are not. The development of an adequate system of governmental reporting is therefore a fundamental task which may well engage the attention of many investigators for some time to come. Here political prudence and scientific necessity unite in an urgent demand for speedy action.

There is unquestionably a broad and fertile field in the use of quantitative measurement for the analysis of many types of political data, for discovering fundamental similarities or correlations of the types already indicated. Hypotheses of the investigator, by whatever method reached, may be subjected to analysis in this manner and in many instances proved or disproved. The strength and direction of various forms of political behavior may be indicated, and made the basis of scientific conclusions. This will inevitably be a slow process, much less appealing to some than swift literary generalizations, although to others the emergence of scientific relationships will be equally fascinating. At the outset we shall have to deal with groups or bundles of factors found to

produce an undoubted result, but in time it should
prove possible to untangle these factors and approach more nearly to a complete analysis of the
given situation. There is always the danger that
"measurement" per se may be relied upon to take
the place of insight and logic, and that the result
may be accurate mathematically but insignificant
scientifically. But this is a peril common to all scientific advance.

Politics, in short, faces the common problem of
passing over from rule of thumb to more precise
measurement, from the art to the science, and, as
in all other fields, this process involves a struggle
of the most strenuous nature along a way strewn
with many failures. But anthropometry, biometry,
psychometry all give signs of hope that genuine
advance may be made in the not distant future toward discovery of scientific relations in the domain
of political phenomena. Possibly the door of human nature is closed by some decree of nature
against the scientist, but it is also possible that we
have not found the key that will unlock it.

6 Politics in Relation to Inheritance and Environment

It may be asked, What bearing have the recent discoveries in the biological, anthropological, and geographical sciences upon the development of the study of government? Here it is necessary to distinguish between the superficial and the fundamental effects of latter-day scientific inquiries in these and related fields. On the surface their effect was merely the adoption of scientific terminology for the advancement of popular causes, but not the introduction of a scientific spirit. Darwinism became the basis for a theory of laissez faire, and also for a theory of state interference,[1] as one chose to follow Spencer[2] in opposing state activity or Huxley[3] in defending it. Anthropology became the defense of almost every race, and supported the claims of nationalistic or ethnic groups, the world over, whether in Ireland, Egypt, India, Tur-

[1] See the brilliant discussion in D. G. Ritchie, *Darwinism and Politics.*

[2] *The Man versus the State.*

[3] *Administrative Nihilism* and other essays.

key, Poland, Germany, England, France, and where not?[1] Likewise the doctrines of the influence of environment upon mankind were employed for the purpose of defending particular environments as especially favored by God or nature for the growth of a particular state.[2]

In these respects there was little advance over the earlier uses of more primitive scientific doctrines, as the assumption of the superiority of the Greeks over the barbarians or the Romans over the non-Romans, or the middle regions over the north and the south, as in Bodin's theory, or of the effect of climate on English constitutional liberty, as in Montesquieu,[3] or of the variations between the characteristics of the dwellers on the mountain and the plain. Many modern writings differ little from the earlier type of local propaganda reinforced by scientific patter or jargon, but the whole

[1] See the interesting discussion of "Race as a Factor in Political Theory" by F. H. Hankins in *A History of Political Theories, Recent Times.*

[2] See Franklin Thomas, "Some Representative Contributions of Anthropo-Geography to Political Theory," chap. xii, *A History of Political Theories, Recent Times.*

[3] Montesquieu found that the superior vigor of the northern races was due to the cold which shortened the fibers of the body, in contrast to tropical climates, where the heat caused a stretching of the fibers and a consequent lassitude of the body. See Myres, "The Influence of Anthropology on the Course of Political Science," *University of California Publications*, Vol. IV, No. 1.

so transparently self-interested as to deceive few. Spencer's theory of laissez faire, while couched in Darwinian terminology, was merely a restatement of the English theory of the early part of the nineteenth century, worded in the new vocabulary of biology which he employed. Much of the defense of the Aryan, the Teuton, the Nordic history will appraise at the same level of value.

It may safely be said that the genuine co-ordination of scientific with political ideas is yet to be made from the rich material that is available. The stage we are passing through is the first and least pleasant and fruitful one of left-hand alliances. More recent attempts of a more promising type are seen in the work of Conklin[1] and Curtis,[2] where there is found a genuine attempt to unite the best results of science with the needs of politics.[3]

For purposes of the study of politics, the chief significance of the recent developments in the fields now under consideration is:

1. The idea of evolution
2. The study of the specific characteristics of racial groups

[1] *The Direction of Human Evolution.*

[2] *Science and Human Affairs.* Another type is Wiggam's *The New Decalogue of Science.*

[3] Significant studies are C. J. Herrick's *Neurological Foundations of Animal Behavior*, and C. M. Child's *Physiological Foundations of Human Behavior.*

3. The development of eugenics as a system of social control

4. The idea of the influence of environment upon mankind

These conceptions are fundamentally related to government in many of its phases. This is true, for example, with reference to:

1. Immigration

2. Education in general, and specifically political education

3. Class relations

4. The relations of Occident to Orient, and of civilized states to backward peoples

5. The treatment of the phenomenon known as war

The evolutionary idea had in a way been anticipated in the nineteenth century by the unusual attention then given to historical origins. The significance of the older doctrine was, however, that it was employed to prove that because human institutions had taken a long time to grow, therefore no significant changes could or should be made at any given time. The historical idea was, in short, the basis of opposition to revolutionary proposals. It assumed a closed world, a completed book, or a world in which changes are so slow that none should be tried rapidly, especially if they jeopardize the interests of those already intrenched in authority. History was seized first as the weapon of those who fought the influence of the French Revolution. Later it was utilized by those who used historical knowledge as a basis for nationalistic propaganda, as the material out of which a national spirit might be developed.

The biological idea of evolution was likewise appropriated, as has been indicated, for the purposes of the laissez faire theory of Spencer, and for other similar purposes, but the general tendency of the new idea was hostile to the pretensions of any fixed class or caste. Evolution predicated constant variation and adaptation as one of the fundamentals of human existence, a ceaseless process of life and growth. Adaptation to environment is the test of survival of types of life and, by the same logic, of types of authority and systems of government as well. The past is not sacred, says the student of evolution, nor in the future shall we find any fixed or permanent system of government that will defy time and change. It is not history or tradition that gives the warrant for the life of today, but inheritance plus adaptation to the given environment. In this sense the theory of biological evolution applied to the study of government is certain to effect a deep-seated and far-reaching change, which has not in fact yet been fully realized; indeed, scarcely at all. For it must be conceded that government is still largely traditional. There are still fixed castes, as in India. There are still traditional holders of political and social power.

There is also implicit in this doctrine the further idea that heredity limits in some manner the development of the type in question. The old biblical phrase, that we cannot grow figs from thistles, has its parallel in the modern biological doctrine of the limitations of human inheritance. Unfortunately, however, we do not yet know much about the nature of these limitations. We do not know what the political inheritance of man is, if any, nor do we know to what extent, if any, acquired political characteristics may be transmitted. It is at this point that the science of inheritance fails to carry far enough for the purpose of government and political control. What may be developed in the future we cannot, of course, anticipate now.

It is at this point that the detailed study of the specific characteristics of special groups of mankind may prove to be of special advantage.[1] Anthropometry thus far, however, has not been able to do more than measure the salient physical characteristics of different races or ethnic groups of

[1] See the keen discussion by Frank H. Hankins, *op. cit.*

mankind. Most of the effort to appraise the characteristics of different races or ethnic groups of mankind has been unscientific, although the study of customs has made some progress. Differential biology has thus far contented itself with the differentials in physical structure of mankind, and perhaps this is the appropriate limit of its activity, and the proper place for the beginning of scientific political or social inquiry. The difficulties in the way of such an appraisal are very great, but the importance of the inquiry for the government of mankind, for the relations of races, for the adjustment of power and responsibility for the advanced and the backward states of the world is beyond power of exaggeration. In many ways the future of humanity for generations seems to be bound up with the successful solution of this urgent problem. If by standards upon which all agree we can measure the peculiar characteristics of special groups of mankind, we shall go a long way toward determining their place in the parliament of man, and toward avoiding struggles for prestige and power based upon assumed and unreal differences of capacity for world-control or development.

Perhaps the day may come when the biologist can tell us definitely what is (potentially) in the original chromosomes, and whether anything spe-

cifically political is there. One more question is
this: To what extent are the characteristics, if any,
in the original chromosome capable of variation,
and under what conditions may these variations
be most successfully made? This is the key to social training and education of every type.

Thus far no conclusive evidence has been produced to show just what are the specific political
or social differences between racial groups, but of
course no one knows what the next generation of
inquiry may unearth at this point. It may well be
that the differentials between so-called "races" will
be found far less marked than between members of
the same ethnic or racial group. There may be
wider differences between various types of Americans than between Americans and Frenchmen; or
between various classes of Germans than between
Germans and Slavs. Upon this for the moment we
may merely speculate or, if we choose, feed and
grow fat upon the rich propagandas that every literary race has published for our perusal.

Closely connected with biology is chemistry,
taking at times the form of biochemistry. We do
not know to what extent the future chemist may
be able to produce significant biological changes
that may fundamentally affect human conduct and
character. The functions of the glands, such as the

thyroid and the endocrine, not to speak of others yet unexplored, may fundamentally affect political conduct, and possibly control may be effected through some of these agencies not now well enough known to be utilized.[1] This is a field which may well be watched by students of government with a view to utilizing the results that may be obtained and the methods in so far as they are applicable to the study of the problems of government with which we are concerned. Bizarre and unreliable as the early attempts in this field may be, it is not impossible that significant results of the very highest value for political and social education may come out of these inquiries in the future.

Out of the study of biology has also come the growth of modern eugenics.[2] Of the possibilities of development through this method there can be little doubt from the scientific point of view, however reluctant mankind may be to apply to human beings the same processes that have produced such revolutionary results with plants and animals. Sparta is a classical example of a partly eugenic state, but its ruling purpose was military strength

---

[1] See Berman, *The Glands Regulating Personality.*

[2] See for clear exposition of modern progress in this direction the following: S. J. Holmes, *The Trend of the Race;* P. B. Popenoe, *Applied Eugenics.*

and conquest, for which end there can be little doubt that the methods designed were pre-eminently successful. Plato in his *Republic* suggested compulsory mating some 2,300 years ago. It is unlikely that such methods will be adopted, but there is abundant opportunity, by forbidding certain unions on the one side and encouraging others, for the cultivation of a vastly improved breed of the human race, far transcending the present type of mankind. At the present moment these processes seem remote, and they arouse criticism and opposition, or perhaps humor and derision, yet no one can study at all closely the progress made in this domain within the last generation without turning to the most serious consideration of the future of the human race, when the methods of eugenics are more fully perfected than just now. The practical politician may be wise to ignore these possibilities, but the far-seeing statesman and, above all, the scientific student of politics in the larger sense of the term will scarcely pass them by without the most serious consideration.

Control is likely in the future to reach a point where it may be possible to breed whatever type of human being it is desired to have. Then we could breed morons and heavy-handed half-wits if we wanted them. We might even breed strange creatures as beasts of burden and toil, symbolized in Capek's memorable play entitled *R. U. R.*, automata cheaply constructed for toil, dominated by more spirited beings designed for higher walks of life. It is possible that we might, as the playwright suggests, mix in a little too much spirit or sensitiveness by mistake or through too great sympathy, and thus cause restlessness and even breed revolution; but that is a part of the chance that the governing group would have to take in such a world. The point is that such a world is on the way, and that it is part of the duty of serious students of government to look forward and anticipate the situations that will influence mankind when that day of control comes. What manner of race do we want? Democrats, aristocrats, a state based on morons, equality or graded inequality? It may well lie within the power of men to answer these questions as they will, fantastic as such assumption may now seem. It is to just such situations as these that the modern biology is swiftly leading us, whether we will or no.

Of far-reaching significance in the field of government and politics is the recent discovery of the influence of environment upon mankind. Always more or less dimly apprehended, the early fantasy has been given much more definite shape by the modern students of geography and the earth environment of mankind.[1] James Bryce in a notable article in *Peterman's Magazine* in 1878 pointed out the great importance of the study of geography for government, but little progress has been made in this direction by the professional students of government down to this time.[2] Geographers, following the leadership of Humboldt, Ritter, and Ratzel, have pressed their studies forward with great enthusiasm and energy within the last hundred years and have made perceptible progress; not all, it seems to me, that has been claimed by the most enthusiastic geographers, but at any rate substantial advance.[3]

They have gone forward to the study of economic geography and still farther to what is termed social geography, and in some few instances have undertaken political geography, examining the extent to which the political location and activities

---

[1] Significant studies in this field are Ratzel, *Anthropogeographie* (1899); E. Huntington, *Civilization and Climate* (1915); *World Power and Evolution* (1919); H. J. Mackinder, *Democratic Ideals and Reality* (1919); J. Brunhes, *Human Geography*; T. Fairgrieve, *Geography and World Power*.

[2] See C. O. Sauer, "Geography and the Gerrymander," *American Political Science Review*, XII, 403.

[3] See H. H. L. Barrows, "Geography as Human Ecology," *Annals of the Association of American Geographers*, XIII (1923), 1–14.

232   of mankind have been determined by geographical conditions. It is not the purpose of this inquiry to appraise the significance of all of these studies, some of which might perhaps be subject to challenge, but merely to show the importance of the study of environment in relation to humankind for the purposes of scientific politics. Environmental relations are of fundamental significance in determining the location of groups and their migrations, and doubtless the character of their political undertakings and systems within certain limits. All of these are of value to the student of government, for they throw light on the process of political control with which he is concerned. They reveal some of the conditioning factors in the problem which politics has set out to solve, and they point to some of the essential limitations in the growth and development of states. Difficulty has been experienced in determining and allocating the precise influence of environment upon social and political characteristics, and it cannot be said that this has yet been overcome to such an extent as to make the knowledge useful for purposes of scientific application to many of the problems of government.

A chief problem just here is the determination of the relative influence of race differentials and environment as such. If the process of inquiry could be carried back far enough, it might be possible to determine what environment would produce a specific type of man, socially, politically, and otherwise. But thus far it has not been possible to do this with sufficient accuracy to make the results reliable. Just what environmental factors produced the Athenians and the Romans and the British and the Turks? This is a problem which geography has not been able to answer down to the present time with any degree of precision, whatever the future may hold in the way of achievement. In short, before comparing the effect of the environment we must be sure that the material affected is uniform, or be able to measure the variations in the material with sufficient accuracy to observe the different effects of the different environments upon the material; and for this the essential data have been lacking.

Would England's physical environment have produced the same results with Hottentot stock? or the Roman peninsula with the Turkish stock? or France with the Slavs'? These are questions fundamental to the determination of the influence of environment upon political characteristics and processes. But these are questions which thus far geography has not been able to answer with sufficient accuracy for purposes of government. In the reciprocal relations between environment and ethnic groups may be found one of the finest opportunities for scientific research, but unfortunately not one that has been systematically cultivated. It is also at this point that it may be hoped to establish again the neglected relationship between the natural and the social sciences. It is quite possible that there are subtle influences in climate or water or food supply that fundamentally determine the disposition of the inhabitants of a region, and which even affect the social and political characteristics of the people; but thus far these factors have not been isolated, and we are ignorant of them.[1] Here again chemistry or biochemistry may develop relations of which we are at present entirely ignorant, but which may in fact have a very direct relation to the character of the political people of a given area.

An interesting phenomenon is presented by the development of what may be termed the secondary environment, that is, the environment created by man. In the development of cities, in the reclamation of lands from the sea, as in Holland, in the vast irrigation works that have transformed various

[1] For example, the attempt to interpret in terms of iodine the characteristics of certain regions.

parts of the world, in canals that unite bodies of water, in the reclamation of waste marshes and swamps of far-reaching expanse, are illustrations of the modification of the environment by man himself, sometimes in a manner so significant as to overshadow perhaps the original environment. The construction of the modern city is a conspicuous illustration of the creation of a new or secondary environment which in turn fundamentally influences the physical, mental, and other characteristics of the people dwelling in the environment. More statistical data are available upon urban influences of this latter character than in the case of the so-called natural environment itself. But are these new environments classed as environment or man? However this may be answered, it is clear that in the future they will possess very great significance for our race, greater perhaps than the original or natural environment itself, in view of the inevitable increase of the power of man over nature.

Of equal significance is the social environment, which is not the direct result of biological heredity, but of transmission from one generation to another by processes of imitation and teaching and training. Customs, manners, laws, institutions may be handed down from one generation to another as special types of characteristic, whether any other

236   types may be biologically transmitted or not. The
child of the French group is taught his local
traditions, as is the Chinese or the Italian or the
American, and is early and successfully indoctri-
nated with specific habits of thought and action.
To what extent the original biological inheritance
may limit the possibility of taking on a particular
social heritage we do not know, but presumably
there are some limitations. Would the English
social environment produce an English type in the
case of the Bushman child, or the Turkish social
environment produce a Turkish type in the case
of an English child, in case the experiment were
made? This is one of the unsolved problems of social science, which, as already intimated in the discussion of physical environment, remains to be
thoroughly investigated.[1]

It is just at this point, in fact, that there appears one of the difficulties that arise from the
separation of the natural and the "unnatural" sciences. For is not man a part of nature? And how
shall we scientifically separate him from that of
which he is an inseparable part? We cannot assume
that man is created wholly by "environment,"
for he is himself a part of it, and he likewise and in

[1] See Graham Wallas, *Our Social Heritage*; A. Korzybski, *The
Manhood of Humanity; The Science and Art of Human Engineering.*

some measure creates the environment just as truly as the environment creates him. He comes out of the environment, but he reacts upon it and modifies it seriously. And as time goes on the modification becomes more and more serious, so that the "artificial" or "modified environment" created by man in turn reacts upon him and changes his characteristics, as his skin, his powers of resistance to cold, his whole physical structure. Is man, then, to be reckoned a part of the environment, or is he omitted, and if omitted, then by what logic or upon what "scientific" basis? This is not mere logomachy, for it goes to the roots of the question whether it is possible to study "nature," so called, successfully and omit an equally careful study of "man" on the theory that he is not a part of "nature" and may be safely omitted from the analysis.

Three principal factors operate in producing the types of political and social traits with which social and political science are concerned: the biological inheritance; the external environment, so called; the cultural or social heritage or capital. In the interrelations of these three influences are produced widely differing results in the form of diverse political types. To appraise the significance of each of these in relation to conscious political control and organization is one of the tasks of politics, difficult as it may be in actual accomplishment.

If in the end we learn just how these forces work, we know how they may be controlled, and then there opens out an approach to a science of social and political control for the first time in the history of the race. Hardly before that time. This may seem like a far cry, but it is nevertheless indicated by all the developments of recent scientific thinking, and the march of science will not be much affected by the indifference or alarm of students of government who refuse to face the facts and the tendencies of the time. The truth is that the race is rushing forward with incredible speed and equally incredible lack of preparation to a time when vast possibilities of social and political control are to be placed in its hands, to a period of conscious control of evolution, or many aspects of it. How will these powers be exercised? Whether governments in the future actually use the power or not, there is every indication that they will have the knowledge before them, and the power if they care to utilize it. The wisdom or unwisdom, the extent and limitations of such control will be the subjects of political discussion and action and are likely to be determined to a great extent in the future by the agencies of political control in the community.

Directly before us lie certain immediate problems, the solution of which calls for the joint consideration of many different groups of scientists. Involving a study of biology, anthropology, geography, psychology, and government is the problem of race and class relations. This finds sharp expression in the determination of policies of immigration, in the relations between civilized and uncivilized peoples, in world-organization. Policies of this description may be and usually have been determined by war, and perhaps they may be in the future. But is it not possible that the combined forces of science may be able to discover a more intelligent and less wasteful method of solution than this? If the social reserve is exhausted in the study of how to make war, of course there will be none remaining for the study of these relationships on a technical basis. But this is not conceivable as a permanent situation, and we may look forward to a thoroughgoing study of this problem in the future as one of the accomplishments of political and social science, when it is fully awake to its possibilities and fully develops its methods.

The problem of war itself has never been scientifically studied. It has been attacked religiously and emotionally, but not with the systematic thoroughness of science. What have natural science and political science working systematically together to say regarding this phenomenon? Except for scattered individual studies, nothing. I am not unmindful of treatises of the type of Nikolai, *The Biology of War*, and of the considerable war literature that has been accumulating through generations,[1] but am inquiring what considerable effort has been made of a scientific character to solve this perhaps most puzzling and certainly most distressing phenomenon of human history. Is war a biological necessity, or a psychological necessity, or a political necessity? Or is it like the old-time duel, an evidence of immaturity of organization? To these questions we have no answer, and, what is more significant, we have not set in operation the machinery for finding out. It is possible to visualize a systematic inquiry into the causes of war, objective and scientific, out of which might come constructive suggestions as to the ways and means of abolishing or ameliorating the worst aspects of war.

Likewise the relationships of states may be facilitated by the same sort of joint inquiry into the fundamental characteristics of various groups.

[1] See P. T. Moon, *Syllabus on International Relations.*

This is the joint task of biology, anthropology, psychology, and government; and out of it might come a far clearer understanding of the essential likeness and unlikeness of various classes of humans.[1] On the basis of this information scientifically established, we should know better how to deal with each other nationally speaking. International attitudes and understandings might be built up in such a manner as to minimize the possibility of clash and conflict, with the attendant misery of mankind and destruction of human happiness.

Fundamentally what is most urgently needed is not the solution of specific problems, however important they may be of themselves—and many are of vital significance—but in a still broader sense to realize that we are living in a world of adaptation with constant reconstruction in process. This is as true of the social and political as of the physical. This is a world of experiment and change, a world in which constant readjustments are being made and must continue to be made in the future even more rapidly than in the past, as man's control over the forces of nature, including human nature, expands and develops and reaches points hitherto unattained. In the new world into which we are

[1] See the study of R. H. Lowie, *Culture and Ethnology.*

fast coming, there will be need for still more extensive and intensive adjustment than ever before in
the history of the race, by just the extent to which
the human mind has penetrated the laws of conduct.

There is no absolute type of state or government. There is no form of law that once adopted
will forever remain the best. On the contrary, the
political world is one of unceasing reorganization
and readjustment. The high type of citizenship is
not that of the man who piously follows the customs
of his fathers or ancestors, merely because they
are customs, but of the one who comes to realize
that he lives in a world of adaptation and begins
early the process of constructive thinking essential
to the changing conditions, retaining or modifying
practices as situations develop.

Natural science is making the rate of adaptation more rapid, and social science will equal this
whenever it is more fully developed. We have
learned to adjust ourselves to the telephone, the
radio, the new means of transportation, but just
ahead of us lie possibilities in the way of social discovery and adaptation that will tax our adapta-
tiveness in far higher degree. It is at this point that
the chief significance of the more intimate relations
of science and politics lies, and here we approach

one of the very greatest of future questions: Will the race adjust itself rapidly enough to the significant discoveries in natural and social science to make it possible for social and political control to meet the new situations which are surely coming upon us? If the new discoveries, made either by natural science alone or by natural and social science in conjunction, are met by inflexible minds dominated by tradition and myth, the result may be disastrous. The new situation might place in the hands of medievalists the forces of the twenty-first century, with their tremendous possibilities in the way of thoroughgoing social and political control of individuals. This would be a calamity of the first order, and one from which the race might be slow to recover.

If we learn how to produce and educate whatever types we will, what use shall we make of the power? If we obtain complete control over the physical and psychical and social structure of the individual or the group, as we probably shall, what use shall we make of the power? Will this signify some new form of political tyranny, or precipitate some revolution against all science as a form of intolerable regimentation, or will it make possible a richer and fuller life for the race? These are the questions I am asking, for they will soon be before us, and they may find us unready to answer in a way that will insure the equilibrium of the race and the continuance of human progress.

The purpose of these paragraphs is well served if attention has been directed to the social and political implications of the modern studies of inheritance and environment, and to the urgent need of closer co-ordination between these various disciplines. The very terms "social geography," "social biology," "social Darwinism" are significant of relations that are appearing more and more clearly as the boundary lines of inquiry are farther advanced. If we examine the earlier work of Galton and Pearson, or read the later and more flamboyant treatise of Wiggam, in which the biologist writes to the president of the United States, offering him the new decalogue of science we observe that more and more the problems of politics are inextricably interwoven with the problems of the science of inheritance and environment.

Now whether the policies of nations or of the world are labeled biology or politics or geography or economics matters not at all, and that question we may leave to the logomachists. But whether the groups of students who have fundamental facts in their possession and entertain different but important points of view are able to come together

and integrate their knowledge in comprehensive
scientific form, is of the very greatest concern to
the whole human race. There is perhaps no consideration more significant than this at the present
time, both from the scientific and from the political
point of view. And if there were a benevolent despot of science, he would compel the union of all the
scientific agencies centering around the welfare of
the race. Geneticist and environmentalist, psychologist, anthropologist, biologist, social scientist
would all be brought together to consider the fundamental social problems in which they are all concerned and which cannot be effectively solved without their joint consideration and action.

Fortunately there is no such despot, and we live
in a world of freedom, but the necessity of co-
operation remains the same. Perhaps the initiative should come from the students of government,
interested as they are fundamentally in co-ordination and co-operation, in management and morale,
in the elimination of social waste through unnecessary friction, misunderstanding, and misdirection. In a sense it may be said, therefore, that the
heaviest load is that laid upon the political scientist.

7 Political Prudence

It is possible that what may be called "political prudence" may be far more effectively organized than at present. By political prudence I mean the conclusions of experience and reflection regarding the problems of politics—wisdom that does not reach the state of science, yet has its own significance. In politics there is an element of time which must always be considered. Action may be imperative before there can be full research and final judgment. Just as the physician may be obliged to treat a wound or a disease as best he can, pending full scientific knowledge of the case or the most effective mode of treatment, so the community is often in a position where it must act—indeed, where inaction would be of all courses the least intelligent and, on the principle of relativity, the least scientific. In many of these instances there is no time to wait for political science, but there may be opportunity for the assembly of the political prudence of the community. Assembly of a mass of information, a series of analyses, a statement of conflicting positions, possibly a common judgment, or, if not this, an informed and intelligent statement of the reasons for disagreement—these are possible in many political situations. Out of this may perhaps come a common understanding, but in any case the material upon which more intelligent judgments may be based. In a representative group of the wise men or women, given facilities for fact-gathering and a dominating spirit of inquiry (or even without it), many misunderstandings, misstatements, half-truths melt away, and the issues are more sharply drawn as to facts, interpretations, relative values.

It may be feared that the counsels of political prudence would be divided, as for example when class, race, nationalistic, religious issues were raised. Doubtless this would often be true, although in certain classes of cases substantial agreement might be reached. But the division would be based upon at least superficially scientific grounds, and so would help to turn the organization of opinion toward more carefully investigated facts and closer reasoning, and less toward defenses of group interests awkwardly disguised. The language of prudence would be the common tongue which they must all speak, however clumsily, and those who made use of the arguments and facts and conclusions would follow the general method of appeal to facts and the efforts at logical or scientific defense of the cause in question.

But if the *prudentes*, the professional students of government and political savants, cannot even come together to discuss some of the fundamentals of political prudence for fear that violent and embarrassing disagreement might show their weakness, should not that circumstance itself cause sober reflection regarding their ideas, and might it not suggest remodeling and reorganization of their methods? Might not the disagreement, even the widest, lead to a better procedure in determining conclusions and, in time, to its strengthening? If the *prudentes* cannot reason together, but merely wrangle; if they cannot co-operate in inquiry, but merely confuse and obfuscate each other, if they cannot even scientifically disagree—then we must re-examine the preliminary education of savants, and start over again on the slow process of growing another crop of wise men with good temper, balanced judgment, and good will toward men.

It is true that when the passions of the community are fully aroused, it may be too late for impartial inquiry to be made or to command any wide influence if conducted. This happened in our history in regard to the slavery question, and in regard to the liquor question. The slavery problem was one pre-eminently adapted to thoughtful consideration by political savants, but the final solution was reached through storms of hatred and violence that devastated the nation and still leave their marks upon our country. Perhaps there was no group of political wise men who could have changed the result, but had there been sufficient political prudence in the nation, and had it been effectively organized, a wasteful struggle might have been avoided, and human life and happiness conserved upon a large scale.

At a later day the liquor question was settled without resort to the prudence of the community, acting in any organized way. As far as I know, there was almost no organized effort to study scientifically the solution of the liquor problem. I once introduced a resolution in the City Council of Chicago calling for the appointment of such a commission of inquiry, and the fullest and most impartial examination of the liquor traffic in all its aspects. But the suggestion fell upon stony ground. In Sweden, however, a commission of inquiry was established, and its elaborate report was a significant factor in public discussion of the most effective course of action. There can be little question that a national or a series of state commissions would have been able to bring together significant facts and to formulate issues in a manner that would have materially raised the general level of the discussion on the wet-and-dry question. But the political prudence of the community was not mobilized for this purpose, and possibly it could not have been done. I am merely saying that it would have been desirable, from the point of view of intelligent, action.

An interesting example of an impartial inquiry was that conducted under the auspices of the National Civic Federation into the public and private operation of public utilities, in 1907. This study was conducted by a board of persons, including utility-owners and operators, representatives of street-car unions, theoretical advocates and opponents of municipal ownership, impartial observers. Two sets of accountants, engineers, investigators were provided. The results were brought together in an imposing series of documents, and certain important conclusions were reached by a practically unanimous vote. This inquiry still stands, seventeen years afterward, as the best collection of material upon this important problem in American industrial and political life. It is an example of the utility of organizing political prudence in respect to a specific problem. A similar study today would be of very great value in promoting intelligent discussion of the problem, and perhaps might develop significant points of agreement.

It is important not to lose sight of the fact that a rational line of disagreement is almost as useful as a rational line of agreement, or at least it is an alternative not to be despised in the development of community intelligence. The disagreement may turn upon questions of fact, upon which material may be developed as time goes on, if the problem is carefully considered; or upon questions of relative values, which may also be studied more carefully as a result of the agreed disagreement.

There are at the present time many significant questions that might well be subjected to the scrutiny of the political prudence of the community, local or national or international as the case may be. The problem of race relations,[1] the position of the press in modern communities, the nature and limits of freedom of speech, the Ku Klux Klan, proportional representation, methods of nomination, the scope of government activity, the limits of centralization, criminal justice in the United States; or special problems such as that of capital punishment, methods of constitutional amendment; or,

[1] The recent study of race relations in Illinois is an excellent example of the organization of political prudence of the community for the consideration of a special problem.

in the international field, the overshadowing problem of international organization—perhaps now too far advanced to lend itself to such treatment.

In the United States very large values would have resulted from the organization of the political prudence of the nation in regard to the Ku Klux Klan. At present the facts are so scattered and so difficult to assemble and verify that intelligent discussion of the basic issues is almost impossible. And in consequence of this condition, statement and counterstatement are likely to be wildly exaggerated, just because the truth cannot be successfully established on either side. In this darkness misunderstanding and malice flourish, while intelligent discussion and tolerant attitude retreat into the background. Where the facts cannot be found, a premium is placed upon dogmatic assertion rather than upon careful judgment, and the most reasonable is overwhelmed by the least reasonable and least scrupulous.

No one can anticipate that such inquiry would solve the whole problem, but it would have the advantage of placing the discussion upon a more informed and higher level, with more of fact and less of unsupported assertion, with sharply drawn lines of cleavage based upon considerations that might be more closely examined as time went on. In any state these are considerations of the very highest value. In the absence of more fully developed political science, they are invaluable to any community desiring to avail itself of the ripest intelligence at its command.

It may be asked, Whence should the initiative come in the establishment of such inquiries? and how will it be possible to set up an agency which can command confidence in its impartiality and its wisdom and its representative character? At times the government itself may be able to organize representative groups for special purposes, as seen in the notable parliamentary commissions which play so conspicuous a part in the political life of the British Empire. Likewise the German commissions of inquiry from time to time developed prudential results of very considerable significance. The national commissions in the United States, such as the Country Life Commission of President Roosevelt, the Efficiency and Economy Commission of President Taft, and numerous state and local commissions illustrate the significance of inquiry under the auspices of men conceded to have the confidence of the political community. In other situations, however, the government may be ill adapted to such a purpose, or for other reasons may be unable or unwilling to act or to act effectively.

Mr. Lippmann has indeed suggested that the government organize its intelligence work in such manner as to accumulate and co-ordinate the facts essential to intelligent national government. Intelligence bureaus, as he calls them, for each of the ten departments might gather and organize the materials essential for governmental purposes, and these bureaus might be related to each other and to Congress perhaps through a cabinet officer appearing in Congress.[1] The same method, he suggests, might well be applied to the problems of state and local government. These bureaus he believes "would deal with problems of definition, of terminology, of statistical technic, of logic; they would traverse concretely the whole gamut of the social sciences." There can be little question that a federal organization of the type suggested by Mr. Lippmann would be of very great value. It would run the risk of going stale, but that may happen even in the best-regulated laboratory, under the most distinguished auspices. In many cities and some states efforts have already been made in this direction, and bureaus of various types have been set up, with widely varying degrees of effectiveness.[2]

[1] *Public Opinion*, Part VIII, "Organized Intelligence."

[2] See John A. Fairlie, "Legislative and Municipal Reference Agencies," *American Political Science Review*, May, 1923, pp. 303–8.

In the end it may be hoped that the Committee on Intellectual Co-operation under the League of Nations may develop an international clearing-house of significance for the world. For informational and statistical purposes such an agency would possess incalculable value, while it might also serve as a medium for the organization of international political prudence.

For in general it may be said that the broader the basis of a prudential organization, the more effective it is likely to be. An organization including many cities would be better than one, and of many nations better than any individual commonwealth. For in the larger unit there is an opportunity for the elimination of the local, the class, the racial basis that has hitherto played so large a part in the formulation of political conclusions and even of theory. We may some day see an international assembly of the world's political wise men, gathered for the purpose of considering some of the fundamentals of political prudence, and together disseminating tolerance and reasonableness.

An International Union of Cities has already been set up, and a serious effort is being made to organize a clearing-house for the interchange of information and ideas centering around more specifically urban problems. *L'Union Internationale des*

Villes, with headquarters in Brussels, represents an effort to provide "an international clearing-house of civic information."[1] Centers are being organized in various cities of the world to provide a genuinely serviceable agency of municipal information.

The International Congress of Administrative Science is another illustration of the general tendency toward the closer integration and association of political prudence. The second meeting of this association was held in Amsterdam was in 1923.[2] It brought together some two hundred officials and students of administration from all parts of the world for the consideration of specific problems in the field of public administration.

Large numbers of research bureaus are springing up in various parts of the United States and are vigorously attacking the problems of city government, especially on the financial side.[3] These organizations represent in part the organization of prudence and judgment, and in part also are carrying on research of a technical nature, from which

[1] See Stephen Child, "A National Agency of Municipal Research," *National Municipal Review,* May, 1923; Charles A. Beard, "A World Bureau of Municipal Research," *ibid.,* January, 1925.

[2] See *Proceedings,* 1924. See also *Proceedings of the International Parliamentary Union.*

[3] R. T. Crane, "Progress Report of Committee on Political Research," *American Political Science Review,* May, 1923.

genuinely scientific results may follow. In the application of the technology of cost accounting and
in the development of statistical analysis they have
made notable progress. Of even greater significance perhaps is the emphasis on direct observation of governmental operations, in the form of
what is commonly called the "survey" of the office
in question. Of importance in this connection is
the work of the National Institute of Public Administration, and also that of the Bureau of Public
Personnel Administration in Washington.[1]

Significant forms of the organization of political
prudence, differing somewhat in the methods and
purpose, are rapidly developing. The Institute of
Politics in Williamstown is an interesting example
of this method in the field of international relations. The American Law Institute, recently
founded for the purpose of restating the American
law, is another striking case of the attempt at prudential organization. The University of Chicago
Institute of Foreign Affairs, the Iowa Commonwealth Conference to consider electoral methods
and processes, are other examples of the same general type. Similar groups are found in Geneva and
Vienna. They all center around the assembling of
men of experience and judgment in a special field

[1] See publications of these bodies.

of inquiry for the interchange of ideas and perhaps for the formulation of programs of action.

Whatever may be the scientific value of these undertakings, and this possibility is by no means negligible, the prudential and educational value of such conferences is very large. If some specific conclusions are reached, even though tentative, the value of the work is enlarged. If agreement is effected upon some problems, so much has been removed from the field of controversy, assuming that the group is representative. In other cases the lines of division are more clearly outlined and the possibility of future reconciliation or accommodation of judgments is increased.

From time to time the initiative will unquestionably be taken in the organization of such conferences by a variety of groups, the government itself, the universities, private foundations and societies; and perhaps some day the professional associations of students of government may themselves set in motion the machinery for this purpose. More important by far than the source of the invitation to the conference is the representative character of the group convened, in order that all phases of opinion may be represented, and the existence of public confidence in the impartiality of the *prudentes* who are brought together. The large educational values involved, the possibility of public guidance in intelligent directions, the elimination of false issues, the possibilities in the way of scientific insights and hunches—all combine to indicate the significance of the organization of political prudence for the welfare of the state and for the advancement of political science.

Inevitably the form of organization in these cases will vary widely. Some will be merely forums with the emphasis on dissemination of intelligence; others will exist for the private interchange of experience and opinion; others will go farther and reach out toward definite even though not scientific conclusions. Others will lean toward scientific reresearch and inquiry, while not existing primarily for such a purpose. But all contain possibilities of great service to the state and to the cause of science in the long run. A study of the actual sources of initiative in public policy at the present time will reveal the large possibilities in the type of conference suggested, and also the superiority of the conference method over the haphazard methods that now usually prevail. On the other hand, although such conferences are not strictly scientific, yet in the course of interchange of experience and judgment sparks of light may be struck, flashes of insight may illuminate the minds of some of the conferees, and out of this may come in the long run scientific value of great significance. So true is it that the truth often comes when it is not directly sought.

Short of the attainment of what may technically be called political science, there is a wide field within which the practical intelligence of a community may be organized and applied to the consideration of special problems of general interest. The possibilities in this direction have never been exhausted or even approximated. To some extent this faculty is represented in the government itself, but under any system there is a wide range of critical and constructive intelligence outside the formal government. A democracy is peculiarly fortunate in that it permits the free development of political association and expression, in other than governmental forms.

The development of political prudence need by no means be confined to formal assemblies of wise men for the consideration of particular problems. Such prudence is scattered throughout the community in myriad forms. It is not as common as common sense, but it is more widely spread than some suppose. Its general diffusion is indeed a prerequisite to successful self-government in any state. Even the most limited political experience must impress an observer with the large number of persons in any constituency gifted with insight, judgment, and adaptability in political affairs. The problem is the discovery, organization, and application of this quality to the problems of government.

With widely increasing education, the whole community tends to interest itself in and assume responsibility for decisions formerly made by the very few. This democratizing process involves and requires a wide diffusion of political intelligence and judgment throughout the citizenship of the state. In other words, the mass of the community must become politically prudent in order to insure prudent political conduct of the commonwealth.

Political prudence is therefore not merely the affair of the savants, but also of the generality of the citizens, and only as insight and judgment are generously diffused will the suggestions of the savants be found to have any weight. Nor will the conclusions of science signify much unless their quality is recognized and appreciated by those who might utilize them.[1]

The basis of this form of political prudence is

[1] "The ability of any one generation to possess the science would depend upon their ability to practise the art and to know how they practised it" (Croly's Introduction to Lindeman's *Social Discovery*, p. xvii).

found partly in sound political and social education underlying admission to suffrage and adult citizenship; partly also in the organization of adult intelligence in such fashion as to utilize to the fullest extent the insight and judgment of the citizens. We still seek ways and means of most advantageously employing that "collective judgment" of men and measures of which Aristotle wrote so approvingly 2,300 years ago. This is not exhausted by the act of voting alone, as is too commonly supposed, for voting settles relatively few of the problems of the state. In every community there is a constant process of appraising the personnel and conduct of the governors and the countergroup of non-governors. Valuations and revaluations are constantly being made in the processes by which the intricate patterns of political control are woven. What Bryce calls the tone or temper of the people may determine the type or form of these patterns, and there is a wide variation between those of the civilized and uncivilized political communities.

Political prudence is seen, then, not merely in the heights of wisdom reached by the few more skilled and experienced, but also in the general level of judgment and insight reached by the mass of the community itself. The application of science to government is conditioned by the level of

this element in the intelligence of the community,
and from this point of view political prudence will
always continue to be a prime factor in the character of government. It will determine whether
and to what extent the precepts of science shall be
accepted and applied, and it will determine the
answer to problems which science has been unable
to solve at any given time.

8 The Next Step in the Organization of Municipal Research

The most casual observer must be struck by the progress made in the study of municipal government during the last fifty years. Prior to the Civil War, city government was scarcely a subject of systematic discussion, except in isolated cases. When the corruption of cities was exposed in the period following the war, the first reaction of the public was not in the direction of systematic study of the fundamental causes of misgovernment, but there was a general demand for the processes of the criminal law, for the awakening of the slothful civic conscience, for the political overthrow of the "bosses." Tweed, the incarnation of the "System," was thrown into jail. Many other minor Tweeds have been attacked with varying degrees of success for a generation. In fact, this battle still rages through the land.

The study of municipal government began with the formation of the Conference for Good City

Substantially as published in the *National Municipal Review*, September, 1922.

Government in 1893. This latter took the shape of the National Municipal League (1894). The meetings, conferences, and publications of this organization afforded an opportunity, hitherto lacking, for interchange of personal experiences, programs, methods, and finally led to the formulation of certain common aims in a model charter. The significance of this body for the practical improvement of city government can scarcely be overestimated. It represents a remarkable combination of democratic enthusiasms and practical judgment which has had no counterpart either on a local or a national scale. The League has presented a fine type of intelligent, persistent, democratic organization directed toward the improvement as well as the strengthening of civic interests and ideals.

In 1907 began the development of special bodies for the more detailed study of municipal problems in a more technical way than was possible for the League. The pioneer in this field was the New York Bureau of Municipal Research, closely followed by similar organizations in Chicago and Philadelphia and a score of other cities.[1] These institutions rendered and are still giving excellent service in their special fields. In the reorganization of systems of

[1] See the analysis of these bodies in G. A. Weber's *Organized Efforts for the Improvement of Methods of Administration.*

accounting and reporting, in the standardization of contracts and methods of purchasing, in developing budget procedure, in directing attention to the problems of municipal personnel and organization, especially on the administrative side, these agencies have done much for American city government. In more recent years, the formation of the Government Research Conference offers promise of fruitful co-operation on the part of these industrious bodies. These activities are largely although by no means wholly confined, however, thus far, to questions of accounting, finance, or organization in the narrower and more technical sense of the term. They have not usually become agencies of comprehensive municipal research. However, in' the specific field to which they have been thus far committed, their great usefulness continues to be unquestioned. Students of government, public officials, and citizens generally owe them for much in the way of practical and technical progress.

In the meantime, many other agencies have arisen in the municipal field, designed for information or action, or for both. The temporary committees of citizens brought together for emergencies have often become permanent city clubs with a social basis and motive. No city is without one or more of these organizations. Nation-wide organizations such as the National Tax Association, the National Civil Service Reform League, the National Conference of Social Workers, the City Planning Conference, the Chamber of Commerce of the United States, the National Real Estate Board have undertaken important municipal work, and others have begun to deal with various aspects of the local problem. Community trusts and other "foundations" have begun to deal with some of the problems of the municipality. Bureaus of municipal research or reference have been established in many educational institutions.

The Institute for Government Research, the Institute for Public Service, the National Institute of Public Administration have recently been organized for research and training purposes. Professional societies of different types have also begun to take a specific interest in the urban question, as is seen in the case of the accountants, the engineering societies, the sanitarians, the public-utility groups, and the numerous leagues of various classes of city officials from general to special. I am not attempting to catalogue these agencies here, but only to call attention to various types in which municipal interest plays an important part. In fact, the number of inquirers and their overlapping inquiries are sometimes a source of confusion.[1] Not even the useful services rendered by the Public Affairs Information Service and the indexes of various journals are able to clear away the smoke entirely.

Notwithstanding these organizations and their activities, there are still great gaps in systematic municipal information and still larger voids in thoroughgoing municipal research of a scientific character. The list of essentials in systematic information is still large, but in view of the fact that more than half of the population of the United States is classed as urban, it ought not to be difficult to obtain these fundamentals, if there is effective co-ordination and organization of effort.

I suggest the following examples of significant types of municipal research.

DIGESTS AND REVIEWS

1. A comprehensive and comparative study of the fundamentals of municipal structure, including the principal cities of the United States. This has been partially done in such publications as the charter digest prepared by Hatton for the Chicago Charter Convention of 1905, in the various constitutional convention bulletins, in the census bul-

[1] See Munro's *Bibliography*, pp. 385–89, for lists, down to 1915.

letins, in treatises like that of Clute; but it still remains an uncompleted task

2. An annual digest and review of important charter changes, whether in the shape of action by local charter-making bodies, or by state legislatures in the form of general or special laws, or of constitutional amendments. The statutory changes in the various states of the Union were recorded in the New York State Library bulletins for many years, and proved of the greatest practical value to those concerned with city government.

3. A continuing study of the practical operation of the different types of organization. An example of this is the detailed study of commission government once made by the New York Bureau of Municipal Research, and published by Bruère under the title of *The New City Government.* At present there is no impartial agency employing skilled investigators for the purpose of procuring objective reports upon the actual workings of various types of municipal institution as they develop. Hence we are at the mercy of observers whose training and bias may render their information of dubious value. Some of the most important experiments ever undertaken in the history of democracy are being carried on with scarcely any skilled observation or adequate record.

4. A survey of municipal functions, such as fire, police, health, parks and public welfare, public utilities, zoning and planning, with a periodical revision of such a survey. Fosdick's studies of police systems are examples of what might be done for all branches of city government. These inquiries, if carefully and impartially made and kept up to date, would be of the very greatest value to those who are concerned with municipal government.

5. An annual digest and review of municipal ordinances in the principal cities of the United States, and also of the state laws having primarily a local effect. Various types of ordinances are collected and reviewed by different organizations, but these are often incomplete in the special field, and are wholly inadequate for the general field. We are consequently left without an index of the great mass of municipal law made every year by our busy ordinance- and law-making bodies.

STATISTICAL DEVELOPMENT

It should also be possible to develop the statistical service of American cities very largely and with very good results. We have no handbook of the type seen in the British *Municipal Year Book* or that of Canada; nor do we have any-

thing to compare with the *Statistisches Jahrbuch*
Deutscher Städte and similar publications in France
and Italy.[1] Financial statistics are not covered by
the federal government and by a considerable number of states. In this direction great progress has
been made in recent years. In 1905, when Dr.
Fairlie and I undertook an analysis of the revenues
of Chicago and in that connection undertook to obtain certain comparative figures, we encountered
difficulties which are now readily solved.

Operative statistics of cities are still extremely
imperfect, and are open to very material improvement. There are very large gaps in the publication and assembly even of the most usual types of
statistics, such as election figures, criminal and
judicial statistics; and even vital statistics are incomplete in many respects. Some of the larger
cities publish statistical compilations, as in New
York, Boston, and Chicago, but even these are
scarcely comparable with the statistical studies of
London, Paris, and Berlin. In many cities almost
no figures are available. Significant progress might
be made by the enlargement of the scope of our
city statistical data to cover already standardized
forms and types which are lacking here. The ad-

[1] See Fairlie on "Comparative Municipal Statistics," in his *Essays.*

vances made by the United States government and the governments of a number of the states are of great importance, but they still leave us far behind in the work of systematic compilation of statistical matter.

Beyond all this, however, there is need of careful study of the question to what extent and in what directions quantitative measurement of municipal operations is possible, useful, and feasible. Are there not fields in which without too great expense we might obtain data of the greatest practical value for the government of cities? Are the very meager figures we now possess the best that scientific study can supply in the twentieth century? Clearly "municipal statistics" is not a fixed quantity, but a developing instrument of observation, growing with the growth of scientific observation and analysis. Almost any extensive inquiry into expansion of municipal transportation, city-planning, or zoning discloses very quickly the lack of great masses of statistical information and analysis which it is quite possible to obtain and which when found are of great practical usefulness. What we really know about the life-currents of our municipalities appears to be only a small fraction of what we might expect under a well-organized system of statistical observation.

For the purpose of broadening the scope of such statistical inquiries, the co-operation of a number of officials, observers, and students would be of great value. A committee of persons interested in the scientific and practical possibilities of municipal statistics could in all probability assist very greatly in the collection and analysis of these significant municipal facts upon which we rely more and more for the intelligent ordering of our communities. Of course no one expects a magic rule to rise from the maze of figures. The "mystic numbers" have lost their sway over us. But every responsible official and citizen appreciates the far-reaching value of a solid fact basis in the development of municipal policy and administration.

It is probable that the federal government might be persuaded to make broader schedules of inquiry if the request were based on the thorough and mature inquiry by persons familiar both with the problems of cities and the technical aspects of statistics. The co-operation between the federal government and the accounting officials of cities is an interesting case in point, showing the large possibilities of advance in this direction. The financial statistics of cities have developed in twenty years from chaos to something more nearly approaching an organized system. It seems entirely feasible to make equally great advance in other statistical areas.

SURVEYS AND ORGANIZED RESEARCH

Beginning with the Pittsburgh survey in 1910, many similar studies in the social and economic organization of cities have been made throughout the United States. These are not of uniform value, but taken together they constitute a very valuable source of information regarding the phenomena of municipal life. They have gone below the forms of government and law into the environment and have examined those social forces without which the process of political control cannot be understood. Many of these inquirers are obviously groping for an adequate methodology, sometimes with relatively crude results, but they are advancing continuously and they are assembling great masses of material which cannot be ignored in any scientific study of the urban problem on its governmental side. Their findings contain many flashes of insight into the inner workings of municipal forces. Many other inquiries made by the sociologists in the course of their studies are of great value to students of government, in that they describe and interpret the fundamental forces conditioning the action of the government. Likewise the organized agencies dealing with the special and practical problems of poor relief in the broader sense, or with medical relief or the protection of children more specifically, are making available many important data regarding the basic conditions of urban life and conduct. They pass from the realm of general theory to the specific problem of the individual case study. Masses of facts are being compiled in zoning, planning, housing, and transportation studies, but much of the material is lost for local use even, to say nothing of more general utilization. Private associations are also making intensive studies of urban characteristics, tendencies, and growth, notably the inquiries of the telephone, gas, electric-lighting, and traction companies. The real-estate boards, the fire-insurance companies, and other commercial enterprises are finding it profitable to use the technique of social science in the practical conduct of their affairs.

There is no central co-ordinating agency available for the purpose of interpreting and applying this mass of facts and conclusions to the problems of municipal government in the broader sense of the term. The Sage Foundation, it is true, exercises a general supervision over the types of inquiry termed "surveys" and has done very useful work in this capacity of standardizing and aiding inquiry. Yet there is no adequate central clearing-house for interchange of information, and for mature analysis and interpretation of all the various types of data collected. Perhaps no such central agency is possible or desirable, but is it not worth while considering whether some more effective device for interchange of information might be developed than we have at present? Even without a central agency it would of course be possible to maintain a general committee or commission for the purpose of such co-ordination and co-operation as is possible under the circumstances.

MUNICIPAL BEHAVIOR

Beyond all this compiling and digesting and reporting of municipal facts, and studies of a socio-political character, lies the deeper question of the scientific study of municipal behavior—a problem of political and social psychology on which we have little light down to this time. We have, to be sure, the off-hand psychology of the political practitioner, which is not to be despised, but which is not comparable with the scientific results of accurate observation and conclusion. An objective study of the characteristics and reactions of urban populations, of the genesis of these tendencies, of their strength and weakness, of their modes of training and adaptation should throw much light on the problem of modern city government. There is no magic formula to be found, no occult force to be sought out and applied for the immediate and permanent relief of all the ills the body politic is heir to. However, there might be scientifically based conclusions which would be of the very greatest value in elementary political education, in adult information and co-operation, in structural and administrative agency and appliance, in facilitating that invention and discovery which should be characteristic of the modern city, itself so largely the product of scientific discovery and mechanical appliance.

Many of the situations in urban government should be studied with the very greatest minuteness and care, without special regard to immediate results. We need the opportunity for detached inquiry which may yield little at first, and perhaps for some time seem to be relatively unproductive. The emergencies of municipal life are so urgent in their demands and the workers are so few that we have thus far been unable to make on a sufficiently large scale those thoroughgoing intensive studies without which fundamental results may not be obtained.

We may say that municipal research is just beginning. We need not look forward to the government of our cities by scientific observation and calculation, but we may assume that cities will be more effectively governed when scientific observation and analysis is more nearly complete than at present, and when its conclusions are more seriously considered by the governing bodies of municipalities. It may be said that we have not yet applied the precepts of experts in politics and administration respecting structure and procedure of government in cities. Yet it may be reasonably argued that one of the reasons why the counsels of political experience and prudence are not more readily taken up is that we do not yet fully understand the processes of social and political control conditioning public action. Many of the aspects of urban government are in large part phases of political psychology, or, as is sometimes said, of "human engineering," but political and social scientists have not down to the present time attacked this problem with even a modicum of success. Until this is done, the full harvest of municipal research cannot be reaped. We are only gleaning a sheaf here and there.

SIGNIFICANT TOPICS

Of great significance in the process of urban government are such topics as the relation between mobility of population and the governmental problem; the detailed analysis of the characteristics and tactics of leaders, bosses, and reformers; the technique of political propaganda; the quantity and causes of voting and non-voting in cities; the relation of social groups to the government of cities; the position of technical science in city government. I cite these only by way of illustrating some of the parts of the field of municipal research in which relatively few inquiries have been made, but which are intimately related to the governing process in the community. They may not result in immediately measurable "savings" or results, but they may lead to a more intimate understanding of the workings of the political side of human nature, out of which may come betterments on no inconsiderable scale. And, after all, fundamental research, whether in natural science or social science, cannot be conducted on the basis of always obtaining immediately measurable results. Farm and factory have found it useful to maintain research apparently remote from results, but which in reality has multiplied a thousand fold the productivity of field and machine, and added to the control of man over nature's forces. The intensive, persistent, experimental, inventive, contriving, and constructive spirit has its place in the domain of human nature and social and political process as well as elsewhere. That "human nature" stands in the way of urban progress; that no finer types of citizens can be produced; that no better forms of co-ordination and co-operation can be obtained— these are not the counsels of the modern creative intelligence which is transforming the world almost as if by magic.

Government does not consist in charters, ordinances, and rules merely, but in the habits, dispositions, wishes, tendencies of the urban population. In the thorough understanding of these factors and in the knowledge of how these traits are developed and how they may be modified, educated, trained, how they may be induced to co-ordinate and co-operate, lies a great opportunity for the development of the most thorough kind of fundamental municipal research. Of course it is not to be presumed that knowledge of municipal behavior can precede the understanding of human behavior, or that we can understand the political or the urban without regard to the economic and the social. But the students of governmental problems and processes may make their contribution to the general progress of science at this point.

There are fascinating possibilities in municipal research that begins the development of genuinely scientific method and is more closely related to such representatives of applied science as the engineers, the psychologists, the statisticians. The great and pressing claims of political education, the urgent claims of practical prudence in dealing with city affairs need not and must not be minimized, but the demands of fundamental research and science have also their deep, if less clamorous, appeal to those who take what Bryce has called the "long look" forward.

CONCLUSIONS

My conclusions are, then:

1. The urgent necessity of providing for a series of digests and reviews, covering the obvious facts of municipal structure and operation at least as adequately as legal information is now supplied to the lawyer.

2. Continuing study of the practical operation of the many experiments in municipal government now in process. For this purpose more trained observers, more accurate methods of observation, and greater co-ordination of workers is needed.

3. The closer and more systematic study of municipal statistics with a view to filling in the evident gaps in our information, and, further, of covering more completely those phases of municipal life that are susceptible of quantitative measure-

ment and useful for purposes of municipal organization and control.

4. The better co-ordination and organization of the now scattered studies of municipal phenomena being made by students of sociology, economics, and politics.

5. The development of fundamental municipal research involving the understanding of the urban political process, itself a part of the larger social and economic process. We need a thorough understanding of the habits, dispositions, wishes, and tendencies of the urban population, of how their traits are developed and how they are and may be modified, educated, trained, and fitted into institutions and organizations of government.

We need not apologize for large requests of men and money to carry forward the study of cities, for half our population is now urban; and the urban institutions and ideals are likely to be dominant in the next generation. America's cities will be increasingly influential in determining America's policies, in fixing the American standard of government. There are times when imagination is more important than moderation, and this is one of them. We need not stammer or stutter when we speak of the needs of our urban communities and ask for reasonable application of the creative hu-

man intelligence which has made the physical
framework of the city to the further problems of
its organization and control.

These paragraphs are based upon urban conditions in American communities, but they are
equally applicable to the government of cities
elsewhere, for the urban problem everywhere, in
Occident and Orient alike, taxes the ingenuity
and resourcefulness of men. The International
Union of Cities, to which reference has already
been made, offers large possibilities of advance in
the direction of the organization of information,
the interchange of experience, the perfection of
observation, and in fundamental urban research.
The hates and prejudices of the world's cities are
less quickly aroused against one another than
those of nations, and there is hope in the more
intimate co-operation of urban centers directing
their united energies toward more intelligent ordering of urban behavior.

9 The Tendency of Politics

It is perhaps clear from what has gone before that the study of government is in urgent need of reorganization and rejuvenation. It should be equally clear from what has been said that the lines of reorganization cannot now be traced by any man or by any group of men. The ways in which future advance will come may be perhaps foreshadowed, but not forecast with any accuracy, for no one can foresee what is coming in the world of science. Physics and chemistry have been revolutionized within a hundred years, and even within twenty years fundamental and far-reaching changes such as none could foresee have been made. In the social field we are far more helpless to predict future development. It is not unreasonable to suppose that even more sweeping changes will be made in the study of social phenomena than in any other field of inquiry. The new world will not be without its new politics. But to what distant shores the quest may lead us, who can say?[1] He would be a

[1] See the suggestive forecast by James Bryce, *The Next Thirty Years*; compare H. G. Wells, *Anticipations.*

bold or a rash man who would undertake either to set metes and bounds to our possible advance or to undertake to picture the unseen world toward which we move. Any suggestions that may be made must be regarded as tentative and provisional in the highest degree. Like the whole of this sketch, they will be set up in order to be utilized by others with keener insight or clearer idea of the needs of the times—a necessary process often repeated if politics is to advance to its proper place among the scientific instruments of mankind.

The significant changes in the modern world directly affecting government were considered in the introductory chapter. They need not be recapitulated here. The problem presented is a double one, dealing on the one side with the development of the group intelligence as a whole, and on the other with the development of special scientific advances; for unless these two are related, little will be gained in the long run. The situation may be considered, then, under three heads:

1. The development of secondary political education

2. The organization of adult intelligence and political prudence

3. The organization of scientific research in government

SECONDARY POLITICAL EDUCATION

The social and political education of the next generation is an immediate problem, more immediate than is generally supposed. If the expectancy of life of a voter in the United States at the age of twenty-one is forty-two years, then in one-half of this time a new generation will have appeared upon the field of action. Consequently in twenty-one years it would be possible to have a new majority with an entirely new political education, with new political values, attitudes, interests, capacities. We could re-create the world politically within some twenty years, were we minded and equipped to do so. We might make the coming generation aristocrats, democrats, communists, nationalists, or internationalists at will, assuming that we were prepared to devote the necessary time and patience to the construction of the machinery for the purpose of social and political education. In the development of secondary education, then, lies one of the great possibilities of the political science of the future.

It is not yet clear, to be sure, what it is that we wish to teach or just what the process of education shall be. Nor is the progress in this direction as rapid as might be desired. Yet, especially in the United States, a vast deal of energy is being devoted to this problem, and it is not unlikely that in the near future significant results may be obtained.[1] In point of fact, much of the secondary education of the world is not adapted to develop political science or intelligence, but to intensify nationalistic or class traditions, in such a manner as to breed war and conflict.[2] Secondary political education is employing the agencies of history and government to make sober and impartial judgment impossible on the part of the generation that is coming on. It is distressing to observe that in the greater part of the world the education of the youth is not in the science but in the prejudices of government, steeping them in special hatreds and special forms of bitterness. If political education is a form of training in prejudice or even hate, the inevitable outcome will be a low state of governmental action and a low level of governmental attainment. Here as perhaps nowhere else the services of genuine political science are needed and may effectively be brought to bear in the struggle against ignorance and bigotry as the guides of human life.

It is of course within the bounds of possibility

[1] See the reports of the National Council for the Social Studies, *Historical Outlook, passim.*

[2] Scott, *Patriots in the Making;* J. Prudhommeaux, *Enquête sur les livres scolaires d'après la guerre.*

that the scientific technique of citizenship and its teaching, when developed, may be appropriated by the community or some part of it and employed for the promulgation of class or ethnic or other special-interest doctrines. Indeed, we may be sure that to some extent this will be inevitable. Yet on the whole it seems probable that the growth of science at this point will also carry with it a broader view of human relations and a higher political standard. The prime difficulty lies in the uncertainty as to what are the traits of citizenship which it is desirable to inculcate. The quest for the criteria of citizenship has thus far been pressed unsystematically and without satisfactory results.[1] We may well ask, what are the specific qualities of citizenship to be taught? Is there a standard upon which there is general agreement? What are the requisite qualities of effective citizens? Do these qualities relate to information, to power of analysis and investigation, to judgment formation, to selfish or social types of reactions? What are the obstacles to efficient citizenship? Are they physical, psychical, social, economic? Can these obstructions be located and diagnosed, and can they be measurably trained and controlled? What are the job specifi-

[1] See my article on "Citizenship," *University of Chicago Magazine*, III, 275; James Bryce, *Hindrances to Good Citizenship*.

cations for an efficient citizen? These are points at which scientific inquiry might be of the very greatest scientific value; and where we may, in fact, look for significant developments in the near future. In so far as the character of the new politics depends upon the group intelligence, it is just here that the most rapid progress is attainable.

ADULT INTELLIGENCE

But if so-called "education" ceases with the schools, it is certain to be sterile. The successful working of a self-governing community presupposes an electorate constantly being re-educated, constantly readjusting its values and its attitudes toward the work and personnel of the government. Political intelligence does not consist merely in worship of the past, but in capacity for adaptation to the present, and for constructive rebuilding from generation to generation. Democracy presupposes not only pious souls with lofty aspirations, but intelligent critics, analysts, adaptors, and reconstructors of government.

A major problem of politics is the organization and application of the intelligence of the community. The political prejudices of every land are well organized. The political greeds, the political hatreds, the intolerances, localisms, and parochialisms of race, religion, geography, and class are all admirably equipped with modern mechanisms. It is feasible, although doubtless more difficult, to organize the common political intelligence as over against the special hatreds of the community or of the world; the common interest, the common fellowship as over against the greed of the local and the special. It is possible to organize the constructive sympathy and the constructive intelligence of groups of persons, and make them effective in the common life. An urgent task of our time is, accordingly, the organization of adult education, of adult information, of the material upon which the citizen's mind may feed. Otherwise we shall be increasingly at the mercy of the boss, the demagogue, a reckless chain of newspapers, the well-financed propagandists of whatever type. In these latter days the situation has become increasingly serious. The demagogue employs the arts of his classical predecessor, but with the added weapons of modern high-geared machinery and the scientifically manufactured poison gas of propaganda. Organization and social psychology have been made his allies and have greatly increased his already formidable power. The demagogue and the propagandist may indeed prove to be a greater menace to the genuine interests of democracy and the possibilities of science than the boss and the grafters.

In what manner the adult intelligence shall be organized may be variously considered.[1] First, it is evident that if secondary political education were properly conceived and developed, a great part of the difficulty would already be met through the general development of power of observation and analysis and through the rise of the constructive type of political mind. Man would be less easily deceived, and would respond more readily to appeals addressed to higher levels of intelligence than heretofore. Such a type of mind and such a type of public opinion would demand and would respond to agencies of information and intelligence quite different from some of those now current and widely influential. Active interest and reasonable determination would unquestionably succeed in evolving other means by which the more intelligent attitudes in the group might best be preserved and be able to maintain themselves in the struggle for survival with others resting on local or special or narrow-visioned views.

It is idle to attempt to depict the form that the organization of human intelligence may take in the

[1] See the interesting suggestion by Walter Lippmann, in *Public Opinion*, Part III, upon this point.

future, but it is plain that sweeping changes are in the making. ⟨The public opinion that rested chiefly upon tradition and custom, or upon transparent rationalizations of interest, or upon ignorance of the fundamental relations between economic and social interests and political action can no longer be reckoned as an adequate basis for a government. It is not impossible to visualize a community where clear thinking characterizes the bulk of the citizens, and where shams and deceptions are so readily penetrated as to make them dangerous to those who attempt to use them. Whether or not one believes in the theory of the "indefinite perfectibility" of the human race, it may be conceded that there is a practically indefinite field for improvement in the immediate future and that we are starting in that direction with a speed and determination never before matched in the history of the race.

The astounding rapidity with which man is mastering the forces of nature and emancipating himself from manual toil is certain to transform human life in ways now little dreamed of. It is, indeed, not unbelievable that in the near future the leisure of mankind will be expanded to limits that a short time back would have been looked upon as quixotic. But now the six-hour day is a subject of serious discussion, while in the most advanced speculation there looms a time when the leisure of men will be even greater than this. A people laboring twelve or fourteen hours a day and without any opportunity to acquire even the rudiments of an education is quite a different people from one which is educated for a considerable period of life, and which works, let us say, eight hours of the day. There will be more constructive intelligence to organize, and it will respond more easily to the call.

Furthermore, it is not impossible that what we may call "political prudence"[1] may be far more effectively organized than at present. By political prudence is meant the conclusions of experience and reflection regarding the problems of the race, wisdom that does not reach the state of science, yet has its own significance. This constitutes a body of knowledge which, though not demonstrably and technically exact, is nevertheless a precious asset of the race. It is the wisdom of the elder statesmen and the savants.

POLITICAL RESEARCH

Both secondary political education and the organization of adult political intelligence are of fundamental importance in the new political world into which we are rapidly coming. But fundamental

[1] See "Political Prudence," chap. vi.

to these is the movement toward the creation of a more effective political research. Some suggestions regarding the scope and method of such a science have already been sketched, but it will perhaps be useful to indicate some of the steps that seem to be possible in the near future. These may be recapitulated as follows:

1. The more complete organization of political information

2. The more complete organization of political observation

3. The broader use of the instruments of social observation developed through the census, statistics, and psychology

4. The synthesis of elements from related sciences into a new politics

5. The development of experimentation through controlled political groups

6. The organization of intensive political research through governments, universities, foundations, and perhaps institutes of political science.

It is urgently necessary and at the same time practically possible to provide much more adequate facilities for the collecting, analysis, and dissemination of political information.[1] Laws, ordi-

[1] See "The Next Step in the Organization of Municipal Research," chap. vii.

nances, acts of governing bodies may be analyzed, digested, distributed in such a manner as to be available to students of government as well as to responsible governors in far less time and far more accurately and comprehensively than at the present time. This is not a task of scientific invention, but of practical large-scale organization. It is essential, however, to the highest development of the study of politics. The student of government cannot be expected to struggle with this vast mass of political material alone, or with wholly inadequate analysis and digest. The importance of the science of government warrants the outlay of far larger sums of money for this purpose than are now available anywhere. The value of the prompt collection of such material is all the more important when we reflect on the significance of the time element in political action and on the enormous reduction in time as a communication factor in recent years.

The organization of political observation is likewise an urgent task, but within the bounds of ways and means now well understood. It presents no insuperable problem from the point of view of modern technique. The fact is that some of the most important experiments the human race has ever conducted are carried on without any adequate

means of recording or observing them. Archaeo-
logical and astronomical observations are amply
endowed, and rightly so, but it is more difficult to
obtain the ample resources essential to study properly the workings of the commission government or
of proportional representation, or of old-age insurance, or of the Russian revolution. Not all experiments may readily be observed, it is true, but some
of the more important should be taken under the
most intimate observation for the purpose of recording essential facts regarding them, a basis for
political prudence as well as for the science of politics.

It may be urged that the cost of maintaining
the agencies necessary for the purposes of politics
would be too heavy a burden to carry. But the
enormous wastes now incurred by lack of proper
relations between nations and groups and individuals is also heavy. It is estimated that the cost of
the last great war was $337,946,179,657.[1] Annual
interest at 5 per cent approximates $17,000,000,000.
A very small percentage of this item applied to
studying the causes of war and the practical means
of preventing it might well have been an economy

[1] Estimated by Professor Bogart for the Carnegie Endowment
for International Peace. Direct costs estimated at $186,333,637,097,
and the indirect costs at $151,612,542,560.

for the human race. A small percentage of the war funds employed by various groups in combating each other, labor and business and racial religious groups, would go a long way toward political research of a fundamental nature. Likewise the great sums now expended in industrial and agricultural research are indicative of the possibilities in the way of systematic study of human nature. We now spend on experimenting with new types of hogs and hens, of explosives and cement, far greater sums than would be necessary to equip and maintain the most elaborate political fact-finding agency that has ever been conceived. In all probability, much more has been spent on the knowledge of the nature of the hog than on that of political man. This is not to disparage the expenditure of funds for scientific hog-breeding, but to indicate the importance and the possibility of scientific study of mankind on the political and social sides.

The existing equipment for the systematic study of politics is a very meager one, far more restricted than is commonly supposed by those who give some attention to governmental affairs. A survey of the personnel available and the facilities available for political research in the United States was made in 1922, and indicated a handful of men at work, and these men unable to devote their time to the work at hand and unprovided with the necessary equipment and facilities for scientific work.[1] These fact-finding agencies will not give us a genuine political science, but they are the data from which a science may be constructed, and they are the material from which political prudence may be much more highly developed than at the present time is possible. If we can imagine a world in which all the more important experiments in every region are quickly transmitted to all other regions, and where the acts and deeds of government are fully classified and recorded and made available to all other governments, and where the wise and prudent are accustomed to canvass such material and draw their tentative conclusions, we shall find that very great gains have already been made in the operation of the governmental mechanism.[2] Many possibilities of difference of opinion will be eliminated, many pleas of those who preach the half-truth or the one case will be ended, and in general the possible alternatives in the determinations

[1] See report of the Committee on Political Research of the American Political Science Association, 1922, also for 1923, in *American Political Science Review*, 1923–24.

[2] See the system of organizing public intelligence advocated by Walter Lippmann, *op. cit.*; Bryce, *Modern Democracies*, chap. i, on the importance of more facts.

of public policies will be reduced to a more limited
number.

Unquestionably the new politics will involve wider use than ever before of statistics and of psychology. Some of the possible lines of advance have been indicated, and many others now undeveloped will be suggested with the advance of inquiry in this important field. There is no magic in either of these types of inquiry, but they offer many possibilities to students of government. Statistics increase the length and breadth of the observer's range, giving him myriad eyes and making it possible to explore seas hitherto only vaguely described and charted. In a way, statistics may be said to socialize observation. It places a great piece of apparatus at the disposal of the inquirer, apparatus as important and useful to him, if properly employed, as the telescope, the microscope, or the spectroscope in other fields of human investigation. We do not look forward to a science of politics or of economics or of sociology based wholly and exclusively upon statistical methods and conclusions. We know that statistics do not contain all the elements necessary to sustain scientific life; but is it not reasonable to expect a much greater use of this elaborate instrument of social observation in the future?

Likewise psychology offers material and methods of great value to politics, and possibilities of still greater things. Methods are being suggested by which much more accurate measurement of the human personality may be made, and much deeper insight into the social process be secured. This work is likely to be developed on a notable scale within the next generation. We may then approach the basis study of the measurable, comparable, and controllable political reactions, leading to the establishment of a more precise political science.

Political science must rest upon a more fundamental basis than "prudence" or interchange of information or experience.[1] It must be founded upon a study of the political process out of which institutions are made, as well as a description of their external features or their operation. Politics involves an intimate study of basic habits, traits, dispositions, tendencies upon which political action is dependent. It involves a study of the action and interaction of these tendencies, of their reactions to stimuli, of their strength, persistence, limits, variation; of their genesis; of their adaptability; of their educability. This necessitates a study, not

---

[1] A history of the process of political thinking, as distinguished from the history of political theory, would be very valuable. Such a close analysis of the methods of political reasoning is in fact indispensable.

merely of the individual alone, but of the group or groups of which he is a part. We may examine either the behavior and traits of individuals or the behavior and traits of groups of individuals with a view to arriving at a more intimate knowledge of the significant tendencies in the world political.

The study of these traits has not been unknown and has in some measure been developed in earlier times. Thus in Aristotle, in Machiavelli, in Locke and the natural-law philosophers, in the utilitarians, there were attempts to study the political behavior of man, to ascertain just what his chief political characteristics were, and how they operated. This was done with especial zeal by the *Naturrecht* school, who went, however, to the hypothetical "state of nature" to discover the simple and fundamental traits of man. These traits were largely evolved by a loose system of observation and imagination, incapable of verification. It would be a rash undertaking for anyone at this state of our knowledge to attempt with any hope of success a comprehensive analysis of the traits to be studied scientifically, or of the exact method of procedure to be followed. We have not yet reached a point where this can be done. All that can be suggested is an intimation, a modest intimation, of some types of inquiry that might be made.

It would be possible, by way of illustration, to study the habit of command and obedience, the traits of conformity, of leadership, of rebellion or nonconformity. The best type of this is Aristotle's study of the causes of revolution and the ways of preventing them, but over two thousand years of additional information and improved mode of observation should make it possible to develop the great Greek's analysis somewhat farther.

It might be possible to make a study of political hatreds and prejudices, as well as of loyalties and attractions. These are fundamental in political action, and they have never been isolated and examined with anything like scientific interest or accuracy. What is the process by means of which these attractions and aversions, so basic in national and international life, are developed and destroyed? Some progress has been made by the social psychologists at this point, but the distance traveled has not been great, and the general tendency has been toward arm-chair speculation rather than toward detailed and painstaking observation.[1]

A study of the elements of political morale might yield significant results. In some ways politics may be regarded as the science or art of morale, but the specific study of this process of adjustment,

[1] See Barnes, *Sociology and Political Theory*, chaps. iv–vii.

of the stimulation of good feeling on the part of individuals and groups in the political world, has never been at all scientifically advanced.[1] Its possibilities have scarcely been touched by political investigators thus far, significant as the process is in the political domain. Interesting studies of military morale have been made, and indeed are a part of the course of study in every military institute.[2] It would also be possible to undertake inquiries into the morale of public employees, and it is indeed surprising that this has not already been done.[3] Here we should approach the psychiatrist as well as the psychologist.

The nature of penalties and rewards in politics is a field which has not been entered. The criminologists have considered penalties of certain types, but the much larger field of non criminal reward

[1] See G. Stanley Hall, *Morale*. The studies of Aristotle and Plato on the maintenance of types of government might be classified as studies in morale.

[2] See the study by Lieutenant-Colonel Mayer, *La psychologie du commandement* (1924), dealing with such topics as the exercise of authority, the subordinate, the influence of customs, the rôle of institutions, the chief, the means of action, the preparation of discipline; also *Essais de psychologie militaire; La guerre d'hier et l'armée de demain* (1921). The chapter on "The Influence of Customs" is of especial interest to students of government.

[3] Leonard D. White has developed such a study in his *Conditions of Municipal Employment in Chicago: A Study in Morale.*

and punishment, or, more properly, of discipline, in politics is still open to the inquiring investigator.

It is possible to study political inventiveness as manifested in various forms. Under what circumstances are the more significant political contrivances developed, by whom, and in what manner? Of this we know very little in reality, but it is not difficult to forecast the discovery of much more material and the much sharper analysis of fundamental situations. How this inventive and contriving ability is discovered and utilized or suppressed is also a matter of great significance in the reshaping of political institutions that is constantly in process.

The technique of political propaganda, leading to the topics of public opinion and political education, unquestionably of vital importance in the government of every community, remains largely unexplored. On the political side, significant studies are those of Lowell[1] and Lippmann.[2] On the sociological side more has been done, but the study is still new and undeveloped, and hardly more than a beginning has been made. An exact inquiry into

[1] *Public Opinion and Popular Government.*

[2] *Op. cit.* See also Tönnies, *Kritik der öffentlichen Meinung* (1922); A. Szirtes, *Zur Psychologie der öffentlichen Meinung* (1921).

the process is yet to be made, and it will not readily be completed.

The relation of political action to some of the fundamental "instincts," if they may be so termed, is important, as in the case of pugnacity, sympathy, curiosity, play or sport, sex, etc.[1] This is a rich field which has scarcely been touched by the political inquirer and which seems likely to hold great possibilities in the way of scientific treasure.

Such studies as these might proceed on the basis of individual cases or of groups. They might cover the physical basis, the intellectual and temperamental basis, the social and economic basis of the individual or of the group.[2] The aid of statistics, of psychology and psychiatry, of biology and of the allied social sciences with their apparatus of material and interpretation might be invoked in these inquiries for the purpose both of minuteness of observation and of breadth of view. For the political, after all, is not a thing apart, but an integral portion, a cross-section of the social life of the community.

The study of sovereignty, to take a concrete

[1] See the significant statement of Bryce, *op. cit.;* Seba Eldridge, *Political Action.*

[2] Very interesting suggestions are made in F. H. Allport, *Social Psychology,* and D. S. Snedden, *Civic Education.*

case of a much-mooted political problem, is not merely a question in logical juristic analysis to determine whether sovereignty is or is not divisible, or is held by the many or the few, but is fundamentally a problem in political command and obedience which must be objectively studied and measured as far as possible. Early students of sovereignty did not ignore this, but they assumed the habit of command and the fact of obedience, as in the case even of Austin, without any critical examination of the situations out of which command and obedience arose and under which they might be modified. Again, the problem of the balance of powers is not a question of logic as finally resolved by Kant into major premise, minor premise, and conclusion, corresponding to the three departments of government, but a problem of a balance of social and economic and political forces and a problem of popular psychology.

It may be said that the methods of science cannot properly or successfully be applied to problems of this type. But that remains to be demonstrated. Even Bryce's concession that we cannot experiment with political forces is dubious,[1] and, indeed, experiments have not been undertaken. Is it im-

---

[1] *Op. cit.*, chap. i. Compare Lindeman, *Social Discovery;* John A. Fairlie, "Politics and Science," *Scientific Monthly,* January, 1924.

possible to devise mechanisms for the study of controlled groups for the measurement of political values, interests, or attitudes?[1]

By rule of thumb we have arrived at a good working knowledge of many political phenomena. The military commander understands the effect of the salute, the orator the appeal to emotions, the boss the process of combination, and all three of them are able to predict with considerable accuracy the effect of their experiments. If you appear before a patriotic audience and trample upon the flag, the result may commonly be predicted. Five thousand persons sit in quiet until the appearance and activity of an orator like Mr. Bryan has lashed them into a fury. The change of attitudes in a group of persons who read Tolstoi as compared with a group who read Roosevelt may be measured with some approximation to accuracy. The attitudes, values, and interests of individuals may be measurably altered by well-known means of education and influence. It sometimes seems as if the only persons ignorant of this fact are professional students of politics.

The phenomena of nationalistic hatreds and reconciliation are written large, and are not difficult to analyze and interpret. In my own case, in 1900

[1] Compare the interesting suggestions made by Snedden, *op. cit.*

I was mobbed on the streets of Paris in company with a group of men presumed to be English. We were saved by the intervention of the alert gendarmes. But on a later visit, in 1918, I found the French and the British embracing each other. If I were to return today, I might find another situation, and five years hence, who knows but still another? When I first came into view of international politics, Russia was the great enemy of civilization, the bear who walks like a man. Later it was Germany. Later France. At another time the British. Again the yellow peril. Tomorrow? These shifts and turns in human political positions are susceptible of analysis, and the results should yield scientific material of the greatest value.

Can we safely conclude that experiments with political processes may not be made successfully? These processes are recurring over and over again. If history never repeats itself, still the basic processes of political control are going on in fundamentally the same manner. To say that they cannot be experimentally studied is not warranted by the possibilities, given the minute and thoroughgoing analysis of situations, the ingenuity to produce the mechanisms of measurement, and the patience and skill to apply them. Certainly the state has more material available for observation than any other institution. The army, the schools, the public personnel, and an array of public institutions are directly under its management, and may be utilized for purposes of experiment if it is so desired. Out of the schools has come psychological material of the very greatest value; out of the army under the stress of emergency came important psychological advances.

A prime difficulty with the study of government as thus far developed is that its greatest students have overlooked its possibilities in the field of experiment. Indeed, both Mill and Bryce specifically denied the possibility of politics as an experimental science. This attitude has had many unfortunate consequences. In the first place, it has left actual experiment with political forces to those who were not scientifically trained or inclined, and thus the problems of political psychology have been worked out under adverse conditions. In the next place, inadequate attention was given to exact observation of political experiments actually under way at all times, and susceptible of much more scientific measurement and analysis than was achieved. This conclusion that experiments in politics are impossible was not reached as the result of persistent effort and many failures, but, on the other hand, without any serious attempt to record the numerous experiments constantly going on or to set up others that might have been made. The necessary technique was not developed, partly, if not chiefly, because of lack of faith in the ability to understand the political process.

In the third place, no effort was made to study the political process by means of the controlled group experiment in which a shifting of the factors may vary the result with a degree of uniformity. Here, again, the failure was not due to unsuccessful efforts long continued, but rather to lack of effort in this direction. Thinkers preferred to cite the law or the gospel or the common custom, or the opinion of others, or to elaborate some natural law or to rise to the heights of logical metapolitics, rather than to attempt experiment with the political process unceasingly going on around them.

It has not yet been shown that politics may be studied experimentally, but it may be asserted that no such use of accurate methods has been attempted as in the case of astronomy and geology, where control is not possible; that there is abundant but untried material for such observation; and that there is a field for controlled experiment in such domains as political education, and the genesis and variation of attitudes in individuals or groups.

It is perhaps idle to carry the discussion of this

point farther at this time. It is sufficient to emphasize the fact that experiment has not been undertaken on any serious scale, that its possibilities have not been exhausted, and to state the hypothesis that politics may make wider use of actual experiment than its students have hitherto attempted.

If we wish to know the genesis of political traits, it is possible to determine this through the study of children. If we wish to study the significant traits of citizenship in various situations, it is possible to examine adult groups for this purpose. We can measure the patterns of conservative and radical, and, I venture to say, manufacture as many of either as we like by proper treatment, physical, psychical, or economic. We can try the effect upon different groups and learn the results with some degree of accuracy. Politicians, propagandists, and advertisers are doing it now with a fair degree of success.

It cannot be asserted that the special qualities here suggested as subjects of inquiry, such as command and obedience, or hatreds or loyalties, or morale or inventiveness, or intelligence or public opinion or education and propaganda, are of themselves scientific elements or forces or categories. On the contrary, it cannot be too emphatically stated that they are merely objects of preliminary, exploratory investigation out of which it is believed that significant results might arise, convenient types that have not hitherto been subjected to close analysis even on the older basis of political science. What we are really aiming at is the understanding of political sequences or tropisms, the knowledge of the basic political habits, traits, and dispositions of mankind, how they act and react, and how they are related to groups and situations out of which they grow, and which fundamentally condition them. These analyses might give us, if successfully carried out, an intimate knowledge of the political process in its fundamentals, such as we have never possessed. Beyond doubt such a quest will lead us into psychology, into biology, into sociology, and who knows where else, before we have run down the elusive clues that may be presented in the early stages of the inquiry. But this way lies the science of political control, as distinguished from unthinking custom, from force, from art, from opinion, from the organization of political prudence.

By more microscopic investigation the political interests and "drives" of the political personality may be better understood, political tendencies and characteristics may be thoroughly explored, and the ways and means of educating and controlling them further developed. We may better know what is the actual basis of governmental power, what are the causes of support or discontent and how they may be controlled, what is the significance of the radical and conservative, what are the limits of group activity, what is the composition of political ideals and their opposites, how the political forces in a given community may be appraised and utilized for specific purposes, how morale may be heightened and developed in specific groups and for specific situations or purposes, how social waste and loss through avoidable political friction may be minimized.

Gradually there might be constructed a new politics, woven out of the new elements of modern life and thought. It would be new not merely in the sense that it reflected new social and economic and political forces, formerly neglected or inadequately represented in political formulas or symbols. We shall doubtless find new philosophies for the new groups, as socialism, syndicalism, communism, internationalism, fascism, taking the name of science and colorful forms of literature. But politics would be new in that it utilized the new developments in modern science, social and physical—of psychology, of statistics, of biology, of ethnology, of geography, of engineering, and of other types of studies that may throw light upon the inner problems of political co-operation and control. The new politics would be a synthesis of significant factors in modern mental life, applied to the problems of government, released from traditional or authoritarian conditions or precedents for the purpose of scientific experiment and the determination of the inner secrets of the political process.

That the methods of politics will be the same as those of physics may not follow, for each new type of inquiry must formulate its own special methods. Slavish imitation of one by the other may not be profitable; in fact, may do damage, as many of the failures in "scientific" social science already demonstrate. For much of this work of developing the science of politics, equipment and resources not now available will be necessary.

It will be found necessary to press the study of political science with great earnestness and vigor, and it may be assumed that personnel and resources for this purpose will be found. The inadequacy of the equipment for this purpose at the present time is one of the greatest gaps in our civilization, and if continued may lead to tragic consequences. The organization of political research will perhaps develop in universities, in research institutes, and in the government itself under favorable circumstances. There are inviting possibilities in the establishment of national institutes of political research, and still greater possibilities in an international institute of politics. I do not know of any greater benefaction to the race than the organization and operation of a center for the fundamental study of the problems in political processes, adequately staffed by students of politics and adequately supported by the necessary statistical, psychological, biological aids, and with of course the aid of the necessary reinforcements from the other social sciences. Aside from the scientific discoveries regarding human nature on its political side, the educational effect of such an institution would be very large, and would be immediate. In setting standards of civic training and in raising the level upon which political judgments are formed, an incalculable service would be rendered to humanity. It is not important or desirable that the political scientists should govern the world, but it is fundamental that they be heard before decisions are made on broad issues, and that the scientific spirit be found in the governors and the governed as well. In any event, we may reasonably look forward to the rapid development of research centers in various parts of the world, particularly in universities, presumably the natural home of research.

And of course there must be a body of scientists earnestly devoting themselves to the great undertaking. The willingness of many men and women to devote long years of arduous and unremitting toil to the detailed study of political problems is a prerequisite to achievement, and even industry and devotion alone will not prove adequate if they slip into the ruts of scholasticism and only wear deeper and smoother the grooves of traditional thought. Experience shows that it is easy to fall into industrious but sterile scholarship. Imagination on the one hand and precision on the other are essential to advancement in this field as in other departments of science. We must have both enthusiasm and tools, often a difficult combination, since the tool-makers may lack vision and the visionaries ignore the precise mechanisms of specific attainment. The political scientist must be something of a utopian in his prophetic view and something both of a statesman and a scientist in his practical methods.

Possibly this development of political science may not be obtained until after wars and social breakdowns have further disciplined the world to a point where intelligence is called in to aid. Perhaps the greed, corruption, and violence of economic, ethnic, and territorial groups will be permitted for long periods to take the place of scientific social and political control. The white, the yellow, the black, and the brown may desolate the world with still greater wars than those that have gone before. The rich and the poor, the mountain and the plain, the center and the circumference, the old and the new may prefer blood and iron as their social medicine, and writhe in agony again as they have done before. And those who worship Jehovah, or Baal, or Buddha may kill or torture each other for the control of the mechanism of political and social control. If human nature is really unknowable, as some say, their struggles may well be more terrible than ever before, as the instruments of destruction are rendered more fearful with the increasing knowledge of nature. Yet there are many indications of the rise of political intelligence, political prudence, political science; and it is possible to plot a curve of progress in this direction.

But it may be said that there will be no life, no heart, no color, no emotion left in the new type of politics. Quite the contrary. The psychologists have not destroyed the vitality and values of education because they have introduced science into the process. On the contrary, they have brought larger and more abundant life to many little ones. The physicians and the biologists have not put an end to love, even though they have brought scientific methods to replace ignorance and superstition. Industry does not cease because scientific methods in the management of personnel or in the construction of machinery are developed and applied. If we knew more about the scientific adjustment of the political relations of mankind, men might live a happier and richer life than when chance and ignorance determined their lot. May not justice and liberty and law have a basis in reason as well as in force, superstition, or formula? Wrong, injustice, tyranny have flourished most rankly when and where the light could not penetrate, in the darker shades of deception, illusion, ignorance, and sham. The dreams of men that they might be free, that they might be recognized as parts of the great political process, the common hopes of security, fairness, justice, recognition will not be less fully realized when truth is known than when its face is veiled.[1] To mitigate the horrors of war, to avoid the destructiveness of revolution, to minimize the losses from costly group conflicts, to

[1] See W. C. Curtis, *Science and Human Affairs*, chap. xii, "The Higher Values of Science."

utilize the vast reserve of human co-operation and
social constructiveness—this is not a task of soul-
less regimentation, but of inspiring release of human faculties, of elevation of mankind to higher
levels of attainment and of well-being.

The new world is likely to bring, first of all, new
rationalization of the new forces of our new time.
These will be rationalizations of new groups that
rise to strength and self-expression. Labor and
woman and newly awakening races will find their
voices, as will internationalism and localism. There
will be other types of Rousseaus and Tolstois and
Nietzsches and Gandhis and Kropotkins. But
these doctrines will be the defenses of those who
have or seek power in new forms.

There will be far more perfect organization of
political information than is found today, and of
political observation as well. This lags, but it
waits only the touch of interest and organization
to catch step with the advance of the modern
world. There will be wider organization of the
political intelligence and prudence of the time than
ever before, not merely local in its scope, but world-
wide organization of the opinions of the wise men
and wise women. And this will bring higher levels
of tolerance, higher levels of discussion and attainment, wider possibilities of wise decision. Toward

this stage of political evolution we seem to be moving with rapidity. I do not refer merely to the organization of the League of Nations, but to the widening of intellectual interests and the interpenetration of national cultures, halted, it must be conceded, in war, but none the less moving steadily forward toward a community of intellectual interest that cannot be wholly lost in the new world.

Finally, the new politics would bridge the gap between art and science, and bring us to more precise methods of political and social control than mankind has hitherto possessed. The new politics would look forward as well as backward, it would supplement traditional lore with experiment; it would be constructive and inventive as well as customary and habitual; it would create and control habits, as well as utilize those that are handed down. It would use the mechanisms of education and eugenics for political and social organization and control. It would explore the recesses of human nature, of human political nature, uncontrolled by authority or tradition. The new politics would not be unmindful of history or tradition or of the "subconscious," but it would also consider inheritance and environment as science unfolds them rather than as power or privilege portrays them for personal advantage. The new politics would endeavor to substitute ascertained fact and observed relations for mere opinion, and experiment for unfounded belief.

This is not the task of a day or perhaps of a generation, but it is a necessary undertaking and a necessary accomplishment if the new world with its new social forces and its new intellectual technique is to be governed under a system of social and political control of a similar type, and if a world of science is not to be mastered and directed by ignorance and prejudice.

These, in short, are some of the elements of a science of politics as distinguished from an art, or from a set of historical and structural descriptions. What final form such inquiries may take it is impossible to predict, and it is perhaps rash even to attempt to set them down here, in view of the certain inadequacy of any such list for the future purposes of scientific advance. What we have here are only crude trial balances, made necessary by the bankrupt condition of the study of government.

The development of the science of government may seem an overambitious program at which wise men may well shake their heads, and probably they will. Yet two considerations are significant here. One is that the systematic, scientific, thoroughgoing study of the political traits of man has never been seriously attempted by any organized group of trained observers. There is no record of the failure of scientific study of politics. Secondly, it is difficult to see how the new world can continue, endowed with scientific mastery over the forces of nature, yet with a government ruling by the methods of pre-scientific time. In self-defense against the raids of predatory propagandists, we shall sooner or later be obliged to turn to scientific study of the basic elements upon which political civilization and advance are resting.

PRACTICAL POSSIBILITIES

It may be asked, At what points does it seem most probable that practical advances may be made, assuming there is a development of the science of politics? This is of course impossible to state with any degree of assurance, but an estimate may be hazarded, taking it as such only.

A more thorough knowledge of the fundamentals of man's political nature might be employed in the field of political education, the crucial period in the formation of citizen character. This problem is confronting us more seriously than ever before, and its solution would unquestionably be aided by scientific analysis of the traits of citizenship which it is desired to inculcate. Another field is the organization for the interchange of information and experience in such a manner as to make it available to all interested persons at the earliest possible moment. Another field is observation of political experiments now being undertaken throughout the world, so that the results of one may be communicated to another. Another field is the development of the science of morale, for the purpose of obtaining effective co-ordination between classes, races, and groups of human beings who now cause enormous losses to the race through struggle of a wasteful type. The war psychosis is one of the phenomena toward which a scientific politics would systematically and relentlessly apply itself, and with reasonable prospect of success. Pestilence, war, and famine have been the historic curses of man. All were originally regarded as the acts of God or the devil, at any rate beyond human control, to be accepted with passive resignation. Pestilence and famine have been substantially controlled, if not wholly ended, and are in a fair way to disappear from the earth. Both these are triumphs of scientific enterprise and patience. War and poverty still continue, but they are equally susceptible to attack by human intelligence, if that intelligence is organized and persistent in its efforts.

Further, with a trained electorate, a technical

personnel of government, the organization of political prudence, and the development of a science of social control, it is probable that a considerable number of valuable social inventions and contrivances would be constantly appearing, to the great advantage of the race. This is the history of scientific advance in all fields thus far, and there is no reason to suppose that it would not likewise be true of the social and political, presuming the existence of a genuinely scientific spirit and also the existence of a trained body of persons to whom the suggestions might carry an appeal and a strong probability of a response. Utopias and ideals have hitherto been so largely the rationalization of particular systems, from the spell of which the writer was unable to escape, that they have possessed relatively little significance. But with the development of a more scientific attitude, less dominated by the special circumstances of the case, it is probable that many more fertile suggestions would develop, that genuine political and social inventions would be encouraged to unfold, and that a scientific attitude would develop in the community itself.

The maintenance of institutions in the past and to a considerable extent in the present has depended upon a backward look, upon an assiduous cultivation of traditions and habits, transmitted to

each new generation by the old as the accumulated
wisdom of the group, and glorified as sacred, logical, historical, inevitable conclusions. Possibly no
other course could have been taken, considering
the state of intellectual and scientific development
of mankind. Perhaps some magic was necessary to
produce social and political cohesiveness, and prevent perpetual turmoil. Dreamers and dissenters
were tolerated or persecuted, perhaps later canon-
ized and given political honors.

But the new politics may be built in larger
measure upon the forward look, upon the inventive and contriving spirit, without disregarding the
previous experience of the past. With a genuine
knowledge of political and social psychology, it
will be possible to create customs in much shorter
time than formerly. They will need less time for
ripening, and the process will be shortened. After
all, the life of a generation of adult citizens is not
more than forty years, and within half that time
the group changes. It is therefore possible to modify materially the whole attitude of the group within say twenty-odd years. Within this time new
values, interests, attitudes may be created by the
educational and social process, *if it is desired to do
so.* In short, we may to a much larger extent than
at present control custom and habit, instead of be-

ing dominated by them. This does not mean instability and revolution, but it may mean a faster *tempo*, a political order resting upon present-day tests of its validity and the prospects of its future usefulness in the given set of conditions. It means less history of the propaganda type and more genuine interpretations of human experience. It means also more prophecy, prediction, inventiveness, as the race sweeps forward in the gigantic experiment of human existence.

It may be said that this is attributing a far larger part to human intelligence in the direction of political and social affairs than is warranted either by any judicious forecast of the future or by any consideration of the actual rôle of the customary and the habitual, the emotional, the subconscious in human nature as it expresses itself in our political activities. I am well aware that many students are able to discover little "intelligence" in the movements of political masses or groups. But two considerations are important to notice at this point.

The steady trend of control has been toward the appeal to reasoned intelligence. The appeal to traditions was in lieu of appeal to force; it was then history and tradition against the club. The appeal to the support of the god or gods was an advance from the use of the club, a form of magic or pseudo-science. The appeal to various "principles" and logical defenses of authority, however clumsy, was, notwithstanding its shortcomings, an advance over the use of the club or of unreason or non-reason. In increasing degree and to an increasing proportion of the political group, the appeal is made to some form of intelligence, however undeveloped the form may be.

To understand the rôle of the instinctive, the habitual, the subconscious in political action is not to diminish the rôle of intelligence in controlling them. Quite the contrary; the more intimate knowledge of the reflex as distinguished from the reflective side of political nature will increase the degree and extent of the control by intelligence. The physician understands better than his ancestors the composition of the human organism, and knows better the relative positions of the conscious and the subconscious, yet this knowledge does not diminish, but on the contrary tends to increase, his control over the organism. As Bacon said, we obey nature in order to control her. We understand the springs of human action, and we use the understanding for the purpose of more effective adaptation and control. The individual who knows intimately the various factors of control in his own body is not made less capable of directing and controlling them than one who is in entire ignorance or possesses an imperfect or erroneous knowledge. The pilot knows the winds and currents and reefs and therefore guides his vessel more safely. The masters of the ship of state are in no different position when they seek to chart the seas of political action in order to find the most intelligent course.

It is easy to sneer at the place of "intelligence" in guiding the conduct of our common affairs, and in so far as this signifies the importance of sound regard for the habitual and customary or the subconscious and unreflective in political human nature, it does no harm; and, in fact, the challenge of intelligence may even be useful. For centuries control over the forces of nature was likewise regarded as impossible, or even as impious. Socrates and Galileo are perfect types of martyrs to fear of intelligence, in the one case in the ethical world, and in the other in the physical world. Pestilence and famine were the acts of divinities and not to be controlled, but to be accepted meekly as marks of punishment of sin. Even in our own day insurance was condemned as gambling, medical dissection as a profanation of the human body, railroads as interfering with the spirits of the ancestors of the Chinese.[1]

Mystery as the basis of political control was strongly urged in the early nineteenth century by many brilliant advocates of the type of DeBonald and DeMaistre. And mystery still has its advocates, *qua* mystery, and its opponents likewise. Historically the glorification of tradition is often the work of those in power, and the attack upon it the work of those striving for authority. Technically, however, this historic controversy has nothing to do with the future rôle of intelligence in political affairs, for the mechanism of control may be used by any party faction or element once it is developed and ready for application. Like a new weapon, it will be used by all contenders for the possession of the social values or the social institutions that surround and support them.

The purpose of this sketch is served if the general tendencies of politics are outlined, and if the relation of the new politics to the new world is challenged. It would be presumptuous for any individual to forecast the future, but it is within the bounds of possibility to show the significant chang-

[1] See Lecky, *History of the Rise and Influence of the Spirit of Rationalism in Europe,* for abundant examples of the resistance of superstition to science.

es in the modern world, social and intellectual, and to indicate which way these changes seem to be leading our politics. That the modern movement is democratic and scientific, there can be little question; that the new categories of politics and the new institutions of government will be shaped accordingly, there is equally little doubt. Democracy, dictatorship, communism, nationalism and internationalism, systems of representation and administration, problems of liberty and authority must be interpreted in the light of these new social and intellectual changes. The decline of custom, fear, and force as agencies of control, and the rise of political prudence and political science are indicated by these new developments. The world will not put new wine into old bottles, politically or otherwise. Jungle politics and laboratory science are incompatible, and they cannot live in the same world. The jungle will seize and use the laboratory, as in the last great war, when the propagandist conscripted the physicist; or the laboratory will master the jungle of human nature and turn its vast, teeming fertility to the higher uses of mankind.

10 Progress in Political Research

It is now over twenty one years since a group
of scholastic adventurers meeting in New Orleans
established the American Political Science Association, and started the organization upon its un-
certain course. Looking back over the days that
intervene between our infancy and this, the attainment of our twenty-first meeting, one may trace
the lines of advance in our undertaking. As one of
the charter members I may be permitted the liberty
of reviewing briefly some of the more significant
fields in this development.

One of the most striking advances in research
during the last twenty-one years has been that
centering around the problem of the modern city.
Research centers, some of them within and some
of them without university walls, have sprung up
all over the country, and municipal research workers have contributed materially to the intelligent
analysis of urban phenomena and to the direction

Presidential address delivered before the American Political
Science Association at New York City, December 28, 1925. Reprinted
with permission from *American Political Science Review* 20 (February
1926):1–13.

of the growth of our municipalities. In no field has there been more scientific and practical political research than here. Goodnow was most conspicuous in this field in the earlier days, and Munro in the later.

The study of political parties has been rescued from neglect and has been made an integral part of instruction and the object of many specific studies, notably those of Holcombe, Rice, and Gosnell. Along with parties, public opinion has been made an object of more intensive inquiry, as in the suggestive studies of Lippmann and Allport.

Political theory has been embellished by the scholarly treatises of our distinguished presidents, Dunning, Willoughby, Garner, and many other studies in more special fields, both historical and analytical.

Inevitably as a result of the World War, but even before that, attention was directed toward international relations, and a flood of important descriptions and rationalizations center around foreign affairs. Many scholarly efforts have been made to formulate more concise principles of international law and to illuminate international relations, as in the works of Wilson, Moore, and a host of others.

In constitutional law many keen and scholarly

observers have appeared, of whom Corwin, Powell, and Dodd are typical. But the observers in this field must struggle hard in the wide variety of decisions that fall upon them. In the broader field of juristic theory the figure of Roscoe Pound looms up large and lambent. On the whole, American jurisprudence remains upon a vocational basis, with little attention to research.

In this period the beginnings were made of the study of public administration. Inquiries into administrative law and organization were already developed by Goodnow and others, but in the more recent period specific attention has been directed to public personnel problems, and progress in this direction may be chronicled.

In the field of legislation significant advances were made by McCarthy, whose untimely death caused irreparable injury. In other directions Freund and Shambaugh moved forward.

In the field of method some stirrings may be observed. Beard struck out into an interesting field of economic interpretation of American political institutions, but unfortunately the task is still incomplete. However, our distinguished colleague, the Connecticut Farmer, as he terms himself, is still young. In the last four years this Associations' committee on political research has undertaken to inquire more closely into the methods of political science. The National Conferences on the Science of Politics have emphasized this, and some progress has been made in that direction, although it is still early for observations in this new field. On the whole, the most striking tendency of method during this period has been that toward actual observations of political processes and toward closer analysis of their meaning—this in contrast to a more strictly historical, structural, and legalistic method of approach to the problems of politics.

Some important aids to scholars have been developed during the last two decades. Among these are the *American Political Science Review*, the *National Municipal Review*, the *American Journal of International Law*, the *Journal of the American Bar Association*. We are all deeply indebted to the editors and managers of these indispensable journals, as we are to those of the older journals. Unfortunately we must chronicle the sad death of the index and digest of state session laws which was for a period of twenty years an invaluable aid to scholarship.

The number of serious students of politics is obviously increasing in number and training, although the striking fact is that the group is still small and pitifully inadequate to the task they undertake. We must record the loss of two of our most eminent scholars of greatest promise in the field of government, Presidents Goodnow and Lowell, who have both gone to that bourne from which no political research man returns.

It would be interesting to examine the fact-content of these various inquiries and to develop the various principles and conclusions that have been established, but the limits of this discussion will not permit such an appraisal.

A disconcerting loss which must be chronicled is the widespread popular tendency toward political fundamentalism. This takes the form of intolerance toward opposing views, and a dogmatic self-complacency intolerant of challenge or rebuke, resulting in indirect, or even direct, suppression of liberty of speech or inquiry. The Scopes case in Tennessee was startling, but the Lusk law in New York was as bad. Only recently in a great midwestern university a former cabinet member was refused permission to speak in a university building on the League of Nations because it is a political question. If we lose freedom of speech in the quest for scientific truth, our descendants will find it necessary to retrace some painful steps over a flinty way.

On the whole, these twenty-one years have

been a period of substantial progress and solid achievement, more than justifying the expectations of those who aided in launching the Association.

However, we have farther to look ahead than behind, and we must therefore turn toward tendencies in the future development of research in the field of political relations. Here we come upon some of the paradoxes of politics. After all our advances, it sometimes appears that we are not fully appreciated by our colleagues, either in the world of practical politics or in the higher and brighter world of theoretical social science.

I had been some months in the Chicago City Council when an astute friend said to me, "You are making progress. There seems to be no prejudice against you because you are a professor. And that is saying a good deal." However, since then one of our distinguished colleagues has been called (falsely, of course) the boss of a great city, thus indicating progress in a practical direction.

And this summer, in a conference at Dartmouth, I observed that my social science colleagues, when they wished to express the absolute absence of science in any subject, were wont to say, "Well, of course, that is purely political." Evidently the "purely political" has diverse meanings.

We are even solemnly warned that politics is

disappearing. I have read with great interest the
comments of those who seem to believe that we
are about to pass into a world from which the
wicked spirit of politics has been exorcised, into a
depoliticized, denatured state—no, not state but
status—in which nonpolitical rule has taken the
place of the outlawed scape-goat once called politics. It is easy to understand what these writers
feel and sometimes even what they mean, but I
am unable to share their convictions, and it is
difficult to escape the conclusion that they are deceiving themselves with euphonious verbalisms.
Whether the ruling authority is called economic,
or social, or political, or by some other name hereafter to be determined, a set of relations similar to
those of politics seems to be inevitable. Whether
the world is righteously pluralised, or unrigh-
teously unified, or otherwise, the astute gentlemen
who wield the power will be the last to worry over
names. What king cares what his scepter is called?
Not only this, but as the complexity of social relations increases there will in all probability be more
politics before there is less; more governmental
rules and regulations before there are fewer.

It is not unlikely, however, that there may be
radical changes in the general character of our
study of government. Laws, ordinances, rules and

regulations, decisions, dictums, dissents, budgets, taxes and debts, capitol buildings, poor-houses, governmental reports, erudite treatises in imposing bindings—these are politics it is true, but not all of it. Whatever it may become in print, in real life politics is vivid in tone and color. Its flavor is in no sense mild and bland, but meaty, savory, salty. It may be conceded frankly that some political discussions have as little relation to life as some treatises, shall we say, in economics—in the earlier period, of course. But politics itself is full of life and action, of dramatic situations and interesting moments.

It sometimes seems that we political scientists take ourselves and our subject too soberly, although I grant that we have never been called the dismal science. My fellow-townsman, Mr. Dooley, was one of the greatest teachers in politics in his time, although he was never awarded a doctor's degree, *honoris causa* or otherwise. No one of us has ever even written a dissertation on the important function of humor in political affairs. Even the delightful Leacock is tremendously serious about politics, about imperial politics. I have sometimes thought it would be worthwhile to write a history of political unreason, folly and prejudice, in order to balance sundry discourses on political theory, and to offset the possible conclusion from that all political action is likely to follow the lines of thought indicated by the great masters of systematic political speculation.

The truth is that we students of politics work under some difficulties. We are expected to be practical, but if we were actually to expound existing practice, our work, unlike that of the custodians of military science, would necessarily be rearranged materially. I was once asked for my memorandum on grafting by an incoming official whose reputation for the development of what economists sometimes call the acquisitive instinct was somewhat greater than that for scientific objectivity, but felt obliged to refuse. We do not teach all that we have learned and are driven to teach sometimes what we are not so sure of. Otherwise we should have manuals on the art of grafting, urban, rural, state, national and otherwise; or courses in demagogery with special reference to local conditions; or perhaps research in bootlegging with criminal law and chemistry as prerequisites; or seminars in tax dodging, with economics, statistics and accounting required; or on deception and intrigue, with ethics and diplomacy expected.

There is, in sober fact, no reason why courses might not be given in many categories of political action as legitimate as the nine set types of legislative, executive and judicial, or local, national and international, or monarchical, aristocratic and democratic. We might have studies in the use of force in political situations, and its opposites, passive resistance and noncooperation. We might consider the nature of political interests; we might discuss the use of magic, superstition, and ceremonialism in politics; we might inquire into propaganda; into the actual process involved in conference, so significant a function in modern affairs; or the maintenance of political morale; or leadership, obedience, cooperation; or the causes of war as well as its diplomatic history and law. We might conceivably develop a wide variety of similar types of political situations and processes, quite apart from the established nine categories, and perhaps corresponding more closely to the facts of political life. The interesting thing about such studies is that while they are primarily political, they have an application to many other forms of social organization; and, if they could be further developed, they would tend to throw light upon many types of social processes. These, I concede, are not orthodox windows, but it might be possible to see through them or others like them. All architecture need not be Gothic.

Some day we may take another angle of approach than the formal, as other sciences tend to do, and begin to look at political behavior as one of the essential objects of inquiry. Government, after all, is not made up merely of documents containing laws and rules, or of structures of a particular form, but is fundamentally based upon patterns of action in types of situations. The political artist is entirely familiar with many of these patterns, and develops a form of control based on them. But the student is likely to be so oppressed by the weight of forms and structure, of rules and rulings, that he cannot look behind erudition and sophistication into the forces, rational and otherwise, upon whose interplay any system of order rests, and in whose reorganization intelligence might play a more important part. The selection of problems for scientific analysis is, after all, one of our greatest tasks, and they do not always follow the lines of established institutions. Problems often cluster around institutions, but it is also true that institutions may be built around problems. Variations in social life force us to revise or reconcile old attitudes or conduct with the new; and here we come upon new problems, new theories, new institutions perhaps.

It seems to me that we are on the verge of

significant changes in the scope and method of politics, and perhaps in the social sciences as a whole.

The relation of politics to statistics I have discussed elsewhere and perhaps need only pause to indicate my hearty approval of the admirable address of Mitchell before the American Economic Association last year. The quantitative study of economic and other social phenomena holds large possibilities of fruitful inquiry, providing of course that the numbers and measurements are related to significant hypotheses or patterns. Even where categories may not be fundamental, as that of price in economics or the vote in politics (both symbols of situations), or are frankly fictitious or provisional, the statistical analyses may serve a useful purpose.

Whatever other advances are made, two appear to be inevitable. One is toward greater intensity of inquiry, and the other is toward closer integration of scientific knowledge centering around political relations.

Most students of government are spread out so broadly over so wide a field that they are likely to get aeroplane views rather than the high-power microscopic examination of problems that is so essential to penetrating understanding. This is perhaps unavoidable in a transition period where personnel is small, and where desperate situations clamor for emergency action rather than research. But in the longer reach of time, closer concentration will come. Indeed it is now appearing.

Likewise we are likely to see a closer integration of the social sciences themselves, which in the necessary process of differentiation have in many cases become too much isolated. In dealing with basic problems such as those of the punishment and prevention of crime, alcoholism, the vexed question of human migration, the relations of the negro, and a wide variety of industrial and agricultural problems, it becomes evident that neither the facts and the technique of economics alone, nor of politics alone, nor of history alone, are adequate to their analysis and interpretation.

In reality, politics and economics have never been separated, or at least not divorced. There is rarely, if ever, a political movement without an economic interest involved; or an economic system in the maintenance of which the political order is not a vital factor. There was a strong flavor of tea and taxation in our revolutionary bills of rights, and there is a definite relation between investments and political order today. The oft-repeated fallacy that democracy was once concerned only with political forms, neglects the factors of land and taxation in early democratic struggles, corresponding somewhat to the industrial factor in our own day.

One of the basic problems of social organization is that of the relation between economic and political units of organization and authority. It affects the character of our urban, state, national, and international organization. But is this economics or politics?

Again, there are many methods of dealing with social deviations—through law, religion, economic and social sanctions. But how are these brought together in a pattern of human conduct? Is this a problem of any one discipline; and are not grievous errors due to the effort to separate these threads without bringing them together again?

After all, it does not seriously matter what this integration is called, whether sociology or *staatswissenschaft* or anthropology or economics or politics. The essential consideration is that the point of view and the contacts are obtained and sustained in the various fields of social inquiry; that twilight zones are not allowed to lie neglected; that partial treatment does not twist and warp the judgment of social observers and analysts. The problem of social behavior is essentially one problem, and while the angles of approach may and should be different, the scientific result will be imperfect unless these points of view are at times brought together in some effective way, so that the full benefit of the multiple analysis may be realized. There is grave danger, however, that these precautions may be neglected and the special disciplines in the social fields may be ignorant each of the objectives, methods, and results of the other, and that much overlapping and inadequacy will result. Our allies the sociologists have undertaken to remedy this situation by a brave attempt to develop a broader point of view and a wider synthesis, and in many ways they have rendered valuable service. But certainly we have not yet arrived.

Still more serious for the student of politics is the integration of social science with the results of what is called natural science—the reunion of the natural and the "non-natural" sciences. For more and more it appears that the last word in human behavior is to be scientific; more and more clearly it becomes evident that the social and political implications of natural science are of fundamental importance. It even seems at times that this is more evident to the natural scientists than to the social scientists, who at times concede the impossibility of more scientific social control of human conduct.

Biology, psychology, anthropology, psychopathology, medicine, the earth sciences, are now reaching out to consider the application of their conclusions to social situations. Their representatives have arrived in Congress, in the workshop, in the court, in the field of personnel. What shall be the attitude of politics and social sciences to these new developments and these new challenges? Shall we hold them in contempt of court, these irreverent natural scientists, or shall we ostracize them till they submit to our laws; or shall we outvote them; or shall we merely ignore them, and go our way? No, we cannot leave them, for alas, the natural scientist may be as full of social prejudices as an egg is full of meat; and not a few indeed are compounded of social views now a generation old and the present prejudices of their immediate entourage, economic and social. If they are to govern the world, they must and doubtless will learn more of politics and social relations. Perhaps they are more impressed with the significance of the social implications of natural science than we are.

We cannot avoid the question whether there is any relation between the psychological and biological differentials and systems of government. The nature and distribution of human equality has been recently explored by inquiring psychologists, and politics cannot escape the examination of the implications of these studies. The somewhat disorganized state of psychology, and the rashness of some of its champions in flourishing these I. Q.'s need not blind us to the fundamental character of the problems that are being raised.

Have modern scientific doctrines regarding heredity and eugenics any bearing upon the foundations of our political and economic order? Childs, in his physiological foundations of behavior, and Herrick, in his neurological foundations of animal behavior, have raised many interesting problems on the border line of political conduct. What relation have they to our quest for political truth?

What bearing have the earth sciences such as geology and geography on the problems of politics? What role does environment play in the complex product of government? At what point shall the geneticist, the environmentalist, and the student of social and political control come together, combine their results, and start anew?

What shall we do with the wide areas of irrelevancy disclosed in the background of much of our social thinking? We are familiar with the economic

interpretation of politics, but are there not other un-
surveyed areas of equal importance? Dr. Mayo
would say, I suppose, if a man is a violent radical
or reactionary, do not argue with him; send him to
the clinic. You may relate this obsession or hysteria
to spasticity of colon, or a disordered salt balance,
or blood pressure, or lack of "relevant synthesis,"
or a twisted experience, or other medico-psycho-
pathological cause of the type so impressively laid
before us, and sometimes with such convincing results. What is the effect of fatigue, diet, emotion,
upon certain types of political thinking and action?
Sooner or later we shall find it necessary to survey
these wide reaching areas of irrelevancy in political
thinking and determine their relation to political
behavior and political control. The process may be
delayed, but in the long run it cannot be avoided.

What is the bearing of certain primitive sur-
vivals of human political and social nature of the
early types found by anthropologists? I am not
suggesting any relationship between a nominating
convention and an Indian war dance, but there are
better cases.

Is it possible to build up a science of political
behavior, or in a broader sense a science of social
behavior with the aid of these new elements, of
these newly developing materials? Perhaps not,

in their present ragged form; but looking forward
a little, there are many interesting possibilities.

At any rate, it becomes increasingly evident
that the basic problems of political organization
and conduct must be resurveyed in the light of
new discoveries and tendencies; that the nature of
mass rule must be reexamined; that the character
and range of popular interest in government and
the methods of utilizing it must be reexplored; that
we must call in science to help end war as well as
to make war; that the mechanisms and processes
of politics must be subjected to much more minute
analysis than they have hitherto received at the
hands of students of government, from a much
broader point of view, and from different angles.

The whole rationale and method of government
is involved in these days of Lenins, Mussolinis and
Gandhis on the one hand and Einsteins and Edisons on the other. Out of what material shall be
woven the political fabric of the next era, if not
from more intelligent and scientific understanding
and appreciation of the processes of social and
political control? If scientists cannot help, there
are many volunteers who will offer their services,
and some may be both pig-headed and rough-
handed.

The particular pattern of problem, the special

form of technique, whether statistical or anthropological or psychological or other-logical, is not important; or what the product is labelled. But this is fundamental—that politics and social science see face to face; that social science and natural science come together in a common effort and unite their forces in the greatest task that humanity has yet faced—the intelligent understanding and control of human behavior.

It may well be urged that greater intensity of inquiry and greater breadth of view are wholly impossible; in short, that the new integration cannot be realized. Alas, this may be true. It may well be said, how can one man know anything useful about law, politics, medicine, psychology, economics, sociology, statistics, and so on? How indeed can he? On the other hand, how can he know about politics and be ignorant of the fundamental factors in human behavior? The dilemma of politics is characteristic of our time, and perhaps our time itself is impossible. One of the great tragedies of our age is the high specialization of knowledge and the lack of unity in central wisdom. The shadow falls over the whole of our thinking and behavior. But this problem is not peculiar to politics; it runs through modern life. I do not know the answer; for either to proceed in ignorance of what we ought to know, or to attain that knowledge seems equally difficult, and necessary.

After all, men trained in one special technique with a broad background of contacts and relations in many others will find their way through what may now seem only a maze. We may find it necessary to begin social training earlier and pursue it longer. Yet if Governor Smith can direct the attention of Tammany Hall to the importance of science in relation to government, as he did in his striking communication of last September, surely the pioneers in the field of political research need not tremble and twitter for fear they may be regarded as too far ahead of the times.

I am not optimistic of any type of promised land of politics such as that sketched by Plato, or later in the broader field of social relations by Comte. These were complacent philosophical gestures conjuring new worlds from airy hypotheses, unverified and with no verification sought. We may be happy in the comfortable obsession that the startlingly imminent approaches to the penetralia of biological and psychical nature will bring with them immeasurable opportunities for more intimate understanding of the political behavior of men, in forms and ways which not even the hardiest forecaster would venture to predict.

A freer spirit, a forward outlook, an emancipation from clinging categories now outgrown, a greater creativeness in technique, a quicker fertility of investigation, a more intimate touch with life, a balanced judgment, a more intense attack upon our problems, closer relations with other social sciences and with natural science—with these we may go on to the reconstruction of the "purely political" into a more intelligent influence on the progress of the race toward conscious control over its own evolution.

In any case, this is not the task of a day. None of those who formed the Political Science Association twenty-one years ago will see a revolution in political or social science, and perhaps our present dream is only one more of those dominant but deceitful reveries so common in all walks of life. Fundamental readjustment is the problem of another and younger generation, now happily moving forward to take over an unfinished work. We welcome them—those who will celebrate the Association's next cycle of twenty-one years—as they take their seats in our meetings and councils, with a brooding interest and affection they cannot surmise. We rely confidently on their insight, technique, judgment, and vision to effect the more perfect development of a science on which we labored long but left so much to do.

Index

Index

Index